W9-ABP-210

TO DEFEND A FORM

The Romance of Administration and Teaching
in a Poetry-in-the-Schools Program

By ARDIS KIMZEY

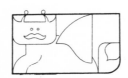

Teachers&Writers
186 West 4th Street, New York, N. Y. 10014

The publication of this book is made possible by a grant from the National Endowment for the Arts.

ACKNOWLEDGMENTS

"Crow and the Sea" from *Crow* by Ted Hughes Copyright © 1971 by Ted Hughes. Reprinted by permission of Harper & Row, Publishers, Inc.

"Aunt Mabel" from *The Rescued Year* by William Stafford. Copyright © 1963 by William E. Stafford. Reprinted by permission of Harper & Row, Publishers, Inc.

"Allegiances" from *Allegiances* by William Stafford. Copyright © by William Stafford. Reprinted by permission of Harper & Row, Publishers, Inc.

"The Heaven of Animals" from *Poems 1957-1967*. Copyright © 1961 by James Dickey. Reprinted by permission of Wesleyan University Press. "The Heaven of Animals" first appeared in *The New Yorker*.

"Vase: September" from *The Back Country* by Gary Snyder. Copyright © by Gary Snyder. Reprinted by permission of New Directions Publishing Corporation.

"The Last Words of My English Grandmother" from *Collected Earlier Poems* by William Carlos Williams. Copyright © 1938 by New Directions Publishing Corporation. Reprinted by permission of New Directions Publishing Corporation.

"Wuthering Heights" from *Crossing the Water* by Sylvia Plath. Copyright © 1971 by Ted Hughes. Reprinted by permission of Harper & Row, Publishers, Inc.

"Keeping Things Whole" from *Reasons for Moving* by Mark Strand. Copyright © 1968 by Mark Strand. Reprinted by permission of Atheneum Publishers.

"Something I've Not Done" from *Writings for an Unfinished Accompaniment* by W. S. Merwin. Copyright © 1970 by W. S. Merwin. Reprinted by permission of Atheneum Publishers.

"Summer Morning" and "Stone" from *Dismantling the Silence* by Charles Simic. Copyright © 1971 by Charles Simic. Reprinted by permission of George Braziller, Inc.

"The Dappled Ponies" from *Coming Out Even* by Campbell Reeves. Copyright © 1973. Reprinted by permission of Moore Publishing Company, Durham, NC 27705.

"The Market Man" by John Ratti from *Some Haystacks Don't Even Have Any Needle,* edited by Stephen Dunning, Edward Lueders, Hugh Smith. Copyright © 1969 by Scott, Foresman & Company.

"A Blessing" from *The Branch Will Not Break*. Copyright © 1961 by James Wright. Reprinted by permission of Wesleyan University Press. "A Blessing" was published in *Poetry*.

Every effort has been made to trace owners of copyrighted material, but in some cases this has not proved possible. The publishers will be glad to hear from any further owners of copyrighted material reproduced herein. Payment of appropriate permission fees will be arranged.

CONTENTS

INTRODUCTION 7

PART ONE: POETRY-IN-THE-SCHOOLS:
ADMINISTRATION
   1. Surfacing 13
   2. Getting It Together 33
   3. Moving Out.. 59

PART TWO: TEACHING METHODS AND ATTITUDES
   Elmer's Glue, Scotch Tape, Poetry and Other Ways
   of Putting the World Together......................... 87

PART THREE: BIBLIOGRAPHY 145

PART FOUR: APPENDIXES
   Appendix A. Obligations of Schools and
                  Evaluation Forms 167
   Appendix B. General Requirements of Poets and
                  Evaluation Forms 176
   Appendix C. "Eating Crow on 'Rent-A-Poet' " and
                  Letters to Schools Included in Anthology...... 183
   Appendix D. Time Schedules and Explanation 187
   Appendix E. An Anthology of Student Poems and
                  Teaching Ideas, by Thomas N. Walters 190

INTRODUCTION

I kept asking myself, "What's a nice poet like you doing in a place like this?" Although I can see perfectly well now why I was there, I certainly couldn't see it five years ago when I was tapped to be in the Poetry-in-the-Schools Program. What were we doing running all over the state of North Carolina, taking roll, making assignments, staying up until all hours trying to find ideas that would work in class the next day, reading and editing poems, and putting together booklets? Only months before, all we had to worry about were images, line breaks, elusive words, and rejection slips. How did we get in the classroom and how did it turn out?

On the theory that hindsight often helps foresight, I have written this book. We now have firm guidelines for the Poetry-in-the-Schools Program. Also, most teaching poets walk into a school at present with a wealth of teaching ideas and plenty of confidence. And whether one likes the methods or not, there are tried and true methods of getting acceptable work from the children.

However, four or five years ago most of this was not so. It is back to that time that this book wanders, back to a time when everything was tentative and being tested, to a time when guidelines were in the formulative stages, and to a time of exhilaration and exhaustion.

This book is a reminder of the questioning we did then and of some of the answers we came up with. Maybe we should even wonder why the program is running so smoothly now. Maybe we should still be questioning and changing.

Most of the teaching poets I know who started with the program have been changing. Like me, they still question some of the "givens" in the program and they are still trying to find new ways to teach. I know that I teach differently now than I have reported in this book. But then I teach differently this week than I did last week. A number of us use almost no exercise material now and lean heavily on imagery, concreteness, form, and word usage. But I may go into a school tomorrow and see something in a different light and then head in that direction for a while.

I guess what I'm trying to say is that I have only one fear about this program, whether it be in the administration of it or the teaching in it. I believe that if a situation is completely calm, then something is wrong. It could indicate that growth has stopped, that reading and thinking have stopped, and complacency has taken the place of exploration and excitement.

We are just beginning to put the arts and curriculum education together in this country. It can be a challenging time, and it must be a time of study and action. It is important, especially now, to look at beginnings, at original concepts, and try to recapture the energy of creation.

I owe a special debt to my colleagues who worked so hard in this program during the first years of its existence to assure that the program got off to a good start. I appreciate their allowing me to share with you some of their thoughts, evaluations, and teaching ideas through this book.

We, in turn, owe much to the schools' administrators who wanted this program and to the teachers who so readily accepted our own brand of chaos in their classrooms. We especially owe our gratitude to the kids we taught, those special human beings who were willing to trust us in all kinds of craziness.

In particular, I want to thank Steve Schrader of Teachers & Writers for believing in this book for such a long time. To fellow teaching poets, Heather Ross Miller, Betty Adcock, Tom Walters (be sure to see some of his teaching ideas in Appendix E), and Cam Reeves for special help with all phases of the book. To my friends who came to cook and do "pier duty" at the river house during the summer I was writing and muttering under my breath full time. To Peggy Payne, my office-mate, who somehow lived through the fall re-writing with an amazing amount of grace and good humor. To Phillip Lopate, a warm, nurturing person who really cares about children, and about those who teach children.

And, of course, I have a special portion of thanks and love I want to give my husband, Jim, and my three sons, James, Brad, and Tabe, who by now know more about Poetry-in-the-Schools than any four non-poets should ever have to know.

Ardis Kimzey

This book is dedicated in love and respect to
Sam Ragan,
teacher, friend, and
North Carolina's first Secretary of Cultural Resources.

I

POETRY-IN-THE-SCHOOLS: ADMINISTRATION

Chapter 1

SURFACING

"The public has an unusual relationship to the poet: it doesn't even know he is there."

— Randall Jarrell

In the fall of 1971, the poets of North Carolina were busily engaged in the numerous practices of poets everywhere. There was the usual peddling of poems to numerous "little" magazines (over 30 in North Carolina alone), the push to be considered for readings on the North Carolina Arts Council reading circuit (which sent poets to read in community colleges, technical institutes, local arts councils' programs, and a few universities), the reviewing of poetry books for local newspapers, and the general harassing of bookstores and libraries to carry poetry books other than those which had "proven themselves." In other words, life as usual in the writing community.

We had at the time three major ways of gathering. We could take courses from Guy Owen or Sam Ragan, from whom most writers in the area of Piedmont, North Carolina had been spawned. These courses went on long after class time and accomplished more than can be acknowledged here. But, briefly, their value can be seen from the number of books, stories, poems, and mere volume of words that have been published by the members of those classes alone. Those two men plus Max Steele and Doris Betts of U.N.C.-Chapel Hill, Fred Chappell and the late Randall Jarrell of U.N.C.-Greensboro, and the late William Blackburn of Duke University, are primarily responsible for the considerable discovery and nurturing of writing in North Carolina. (Of course we have a great literary tradition to follow with writers like Reynolds Price and Thomas Wolfe, just to mention two of the famous sons.)

The second way to get together was to attend the North Carolina Writers' Conference, traditionally held the last weekend in July, and the place to go to get the most amount of mileage on the past year's accomplishments. The Conference, at the time, was open only by invitation and only to those who had had a book published. This caused considerable controversy, particularly among the younger writers who had had short stories and poems published in places of great import but who had to be invited to the Conference year after year by someone else because of zero book publication. When they got there they often found themselves considered young upstarts "who write that disjointed, no conclusion stuff" by older, more established writers, some of whom were there by virtue of several vanity publications or an established newspaper column. This is the ultimate of opposites of course. Mostly, it was hard-working writers who had had an authentically good book published, and the young writers were generally brought to the conference by these good writers who wanted the young to have their chance to look over the other writers in North Carolina. Since then, things have changed considerably and the Conference is more modern in its approach and more encompassing in its reach.

The third and most joyous way of gathering was at autographing parties for friends. If the book was fiction lots of people were there, in addition to the regulars. If the book was poetry, then just poetry people and assorted friends under duress were there. Occasionally, there would be a real blast for an important book by a special person. It was at such a party for a friend (and my teacher), Sam Ragan, that I heard the first rumors of teaching poetry in the schools. Sam was at that time North Carolina's first Secretary of Cultural Resources. The North Carolina Arts Council was only one of many state agencies under his wing. It was the Council and Sam who were instrumental in bringing the poetry program to North Carolina by way of money and encouragement from the National Endowment for the Arts. It was thought by rank and file poets like me that when and if this historical and meaningful task was decided upon, then only those most established and published poets would carry the banner.

I had forgotten the whole thing when I picked up the newspaper one evening in September and saw that a committee appointed by the Arts Council had named 26 poets to be teachers in the first North Carolina Poetry-in-the-Schools Program. The article included my name among those chosen. The delight and prestige vanished pretty quickly under a sheet of panic. Despite having three boys in residence, I didn't really know that much about large groups of children. And how does one teach poetry and where and when. Calls to friends on the list got me nowhere. Everybody was in the dark.

Fortunately for all, it wasn't long before we got some information on the situation. The State Department of Public Instruction was in charge of administering the program with a member of the Cultural Arts Division, Dr. Melvin Good, as coordinator. Letters had already been sent to the school superintendents back in the summer heralding the new program. As a result, the same committee that chose the poets also chose the schools where the program would go. They simply decided to send the poets for a week into the first 29 schools who applied. So many other schools had also applied that it was decided to hire two poets, Heather Miller and Randall Ackley, to go into schools to do one- or two-day workshops.

As it turned out, some of the poets who were originally chosen couldn't go into the schools for one reason or another. So, in the end, several of us got to go to two schools. Later in the year the one- and two-day jobs overcame even the fantastic stamina of Miller and Ackley, so I stepped in and did some of those too.

Immediately, the whole operation was dubbed "Rent-a-Poet" by one of our caustic literary page newsmen in the state. His contentions were that it was not well organized, that some of the poets chosen were not "poets," some of those who were were not teachers, and some teachers who were also poets were not chosen...in other words, the whole mess was more than slightly ridiculous and inbred and ill-bred.

In addition, the poets who had to go into the schools were still shaking and asking more shrilly all the time...what in the ever-loving hell are we supposed to do with all them kids! And the schools who had been notified that they had a poet didn't know what to do with it. Everyone was in such an uproar that it was obvious to the powers that be that some sort of sustaining conference was in order.

In the meantime, we had all received our assignments, plus some information on the program in general from Len Randolph, Director of Literary Programs of the National Endowment, plus a handout from Poets and Writers of New York which went to the schools, on the general care and feeding of poets. We also knew that we'd all be together at a conference in January before we started our stints in the schools. I would have been feeling considerably better if I hadn't been assigned to two schools at the opposite ends of the teaching spectrum, an elementary school in Asheboro and a high school in

Salisbury. As it turned out, it was for the best, like eating your carrots.

By the time the conference actually came about most of us were feeling a lot better. We had put our heads together on several occasions to discuss this animal we were about to approach. Fortunately we had found out about Kenneth Koch's *Wishes Lies and Dreams* and most of us had absorbed it to the point of memory. Of course, it wasn't carried locally and, as I recall, Guy Owen had the only available copy, it having been given to him by the South Carolina people when he worked in their program. Finally my copy arrived from my favorite Washington, D.C. bookstore. It was very fortunate that we had this book early because by the time the conference arrived on the scene, most of us were due in the schools in several weeks.

About Kenneth Koch . . . Many of the poets were like me and used his methods almost exclusively in elementary schools that first year. A few didn't like his ideas at all and never have used them. Since that first year (and really even then) my methods have become more my own, but my lord, do people realize what chaos would have reigned about the country four years ago without Kenneth Koch? Do they realize what points of departure he has given the ones of us who teach poetry and stay in the classroom all the time?

Conference time came and most of the poets were there in addition to representatives from most of the schools. Jim Hall, Cultural Arts Division Head of the State Department of Public Instruction, and Sam Ragan, gave the opening statements. Mr. Hall presented a slide program called "A Child of Crisis" which was very interesting and the first glimmer of the field of education that some of us had ever had.

At lunch we were supposed to have met with people from our schools, but we didn't know that and most of us wandered off with other poets to see what their ideas were about our new undertaking. This was quickly remedied by an announcement after we got back and the ones of us who had not met with our people did so following the afternoon session. As it turned out they didn't really know much more than we did and we drew such a blank about scheduling the classes that later this caused lots of trouble.

Len Randolph came to our conference and gave a very moving talk about his work with the Indians in the field of self-expression. Also we saw the film, "Wishes, Lies, and Dreams," with Kenneth Koch as the star. It seemed easy enough the way he did it, but there

16

wasn't anyone there dense enough not to realize that the easy rapport he had with the kids came from long association with them. Clearly we would have to fight a bit harder in our one short week.

Mel Good, coordinator for the project, then discussed things like evaluations, expense accounts, and getting representative student work. He suggested that there was a possibility that eventually some compilation of the work from over the state would be done. It was apparent to me the next spring when I took over running the program that not many people were listening at that point. Also, everybody interpreted the gathering of student work in a different manner. Len Randolph said in an answer to a question about it that each child should have something duplicated and distributed if possible in the school and that copies of this should be sent to the office in Raleigh. Many did not understand. He also stated that the poets should not be expected to teach more than four classes a day, and this definitely was not taken as the gospel as we will see later. All in all, it appeared that we were to go to a school, teach five days, give a teacher workshop, try to help get student work together, copied, distributed, and then leave.

That night a poetry reading was held and the participating poets read their work. A few had had a "few" and the result made it immediately apparent that this was going to be an interesting year. Mel Good paled as a few choice words flew by him and I knew he was imagining this taking place in innocent classrooms all over the state and him on the corner selling newspapers. We all got together afterwards and it was also apparent that the ones who had taught creative writing in the colleges would have an advantage over the ones of us who had not taught anything anywhere. For one thing, they could get up and speak without fainting. They were reasonably sure that the students wouldn't laugh or walk out. They had SOMETHING TO SAY.

February finally came and we were off. From the mountains to the sea and all those other good directions, we roved and poeted, a nervous excited band, sometimes struck down by fear and icy roads and uptight teachers, but for the most part a pretty successful group. For one thing the local newspapers were delighted to have something as exotic as poetry to write about, and to have a real live poet in captivity in a local school was gangbusters. The press probably printed more misquotes, more errors, more misknowledge about this particular program than ever before or since, but by God, they printed something about poetry and teaching and it got across. To make it short, we got rave notices all over the state, with lots of pictures and space.

Personally I was undergoing a crisis of sorts. The first time I left home to go teach in my elementary school was the first time I had ever left home period. I put my suitcases, books, teaching materials, tranquilizers, and Diet Dr. Peppers in the back seat, and took off down the road for the first time all by myself, without family or friends, going to a strange place with strange people and surroundings . . . never having done any of this before, never teaching, anything. Looking back on it, it's a wonder I didn't have a nervous breakdown before I'd gone ten miles. I kept together by sheer will and the knowledge that I'd get paid for what I was doing, whatever that turned out to be!

Things couldn't have gone any better. Later, and many schools behind me and many strange experiences, I realized what a fluke that first good experience was. The whole school was geared up for my coming. The principal, teachers, librarian, students, all were aware that the "poet" was "in residence." I also had a great place to stay, a rooming house where I wouldn't get scared, and very kind people who kept inviting me down for breakfast every morning and kept making sure I wasn't lonely. I called home every night or home called me. On my birthday, which occurred while I was there, my husband sent me a dozen red roses, to the school.

My first days in the classroom were perfect. I talked, the children wrote, the teachers were happy with the results, and the principal was delighted. He was particularly delighted to get me to agree to an extra class, two assemblies for the lower grades and the students I didn't get to see, and to do a night PTA meeting. Euphoria does many things to people, such as render them incapable of making reasonable decisions. In addition to all that, I was spending my nights reading all the poems from that day and marking the ones I thought ought to be reproduced in the booklet that the school was doing. The next day, the school secretary (and finally some mothers) would type what I had marked the night before. So every day brought more samples of the work. At the end of the week, I spent the last night I was in town checking rolls against what had already been typed to make sure that every child was represented with something. The last day, I stayed after school to finish up this job. Later, I found much better ways of doing this, but it remains one of the worst jobs, making sure that the kid's work gets out to all the school in some form printed up and that every child has something there. It was important to me then and it has remained important, mainly because it means more to the children than almost anything else you can do for them.

Two things the kids did that week were interesting to me. The first day I was there I had a boy in the fourth grade who politely informed me in the hall that poetry was awful and dumb and he didn't intend to write a word. Also at that point, he opened his hand to show me a very black, very plastic spider, and asked me if I liked spiders. I told him they were the thing I liked least in the world and in no uncertain terms I would get violent if anyone should put such a creature near me. Needless to say, every day when I came into the room that spider would wind up somewhere nearby, on my purse, on my papers, in my books. Every time I would shriek and sputter and give dire warnings. The teacher assured me it was because he liked me. There's nothing like the affection of a ten year old to give you the crazies. However, as the week progressed, this boy of the spider wrote some of the best poetry written. The last day I was determined not to react at all to the spider. After all, I had gotten kind of used to the wretched thing. When it appeared on the desk I very calmly picked it up and returned it to the owner. How come you're not scared of it any more he wanted to know. I've gotten used to it I replied and I even kind of like it now. As I left the class for the last time and walked down the hall the boy ran and caught up with me. Here, he said, holding out his hand, I kind of like poetry now too . . . now that I'm used to it. Want my spider to remember me by? Yes, I did, and he ran back to his class and I stood there with funny feelings. The spider has a permanent home on my desk and everyone who knows about my phobia thinks it's a pretty strange arrangement!

It was close to Valentine's Day when I left and one of the rooms decided to have a going away heart of candy for me with everyone doing valentines to go with it. This was the very room that I'd had the most trouble convincing that rhyme really slows you down when you're writing. I was amazed at the inventiveness with which they all did their valentines without a rhyme in the bunch. It was a good present.

It was on the way home that I realized how completely exhausted I was, but I felt absolutely great . . . high . . . I floated home. I'd had a peak week. Everything went as planned and even that which didn't turned out all right. I made myself a few mental notes about things I'd never do again and a few about how I'd do things differently, but on the whole life was good and I wouldn't even worry about the high school coming up.

I touched base that next week with a number of my friends and found that they'd had pretty heady experiences too. The problems were minor and just beginning to emerge. Strangely enough these minor ones were the big ones by the year's end. Mainly small conflicts about the poet's role and where were the teachers supposed to fit in and which kids were to come to the classes and how long was the poet to teach.

The week I spent in Salisbury High School was one of the best weeks I've ever spent in a school. I organized my time to the teeth and Ruth Young, the teacher in charge of and responsible for my visit, had super organized the week. It was a pleasant week socially as well. I shared a motel room with another poet in the program, Sally Buckner, who was working a few miles away in another school. As it turned out, when we arrived at the motel they told us they had overbooked and we had no room. We tried a few other motels before it occurred to us that there was a convention in town and every room was apparently taken.

This is where it comes in handy having made your contact with the person in charge earlier. Ruth and her husband had come to my home in Raleigh and we'd talked over our plans for the week at her school at the time of the conference. Now I had to call her and tell her that I was there with no place to stay. I realized many schools later that this type of thing is to be expected. Nothing ever goes without a hitch of some kind. In any case it only took one call from them to someone in politics there to uncover us a lovely room at the best motel in town.

When I got to the school Monday the kids were so excited you could feel it in the air. In the meantime I was so nervous I thought I might pass out. High school, for the lord's sake . . . the only high school students I knew were babysitters. Were they hostile? Would they laugh? Would they know more than I did? Would it be apparent that I would do anything to keep them happy for a week so I could get out of there. Oh, why had I come and what in the hell was I doing this far from home with a roomful of wise-looking kids. I told myself in my best motherly fashion, it's going to be ALL RIGHT, took a deep breath and found my notes and put my name on the board and we were off.

As it turned out almost every kid in the school had wanted to be in the poetry class and it was considered an honor to be in it at all. Everyone who wanted to be in the class had put his name in a hat (literally).

Thirty from each class (two classes of juniors) had been chosen. I met with four fifty-minute classes a day. I had two back to back in the morning, a coffee break, another class, lunch, and a fourth class near the end of the school day.

The school had a strong literary program with emphasis on creative writing, so they were set up and ready to move into contemporary poetry. Ruth and I had strong reverse feelings about rhyme and meter at that time, but to her credit she never tried to discredit me or anything I did in the classroom. Other poets were not so lucky. I also had a long talk with the librarian trying to suggest some contemporary poetry anthologies for her to order. There were none in the school at all. This whole situation was not all that strange. Other schools were the same that first year and most were not even open to suggestion. More about this later as well as some of the teaching methods I used with the high schoolers.

In the meantime back in the classroom the kids were great. The teachers were going through accreditation, which must be like going through a difficult pregnancy. In any case I never saw any of them except in the lounge and even then they were muttering over long sheets of paper and lots of forms. There was a tea one afternoon after school and I was asked to speak for about five minutes on what I was doing, and I did, and everyone went home happy with the "teacher workshop" obligation fulfilled.

As the teachers got weaker and weaker near the end of the week, it occurred to me that I had about a third again as many students as I started out with. Surely all those requests I had said okay to about bringing a friend had not garnered me this many more kids. But it had. They'd appear with permission slips in hand and I'd sign them and the same kids were there all day from one class to another and soon they were sitting on the floor and on the window ledges and everywhere. We'd close the door and try to be quiet and they'd listen to the records I brought and the ones they brought and we'd listen to the poems I brought and the ones they brought and we'd write and write and write. And I still don't know what happened that week except the kids knew they had to be "good and quiet" while their teachers were going through so much hell and I was there and the room was there and so why not write poems? The last day one girl even brought her dog to class all day and nobody even asked about it from the office. I think the moral of this story is to come to a school during the last week it's going through accreditation.

The last hour of the last day the videotape crew from the school came in and wanted to tape a class. They wanted to know if we wanted to get prepared and all that. By that time I was so pole-axed and the kids were so relaxed that I said just start when you're ready and they did and we got some good footage with lots of laughing and in-jokes and poems read and general good feelings expressed.

I went home thinking every school was going to be a snap. Exhausting, yes, but good programs and well-run and appreciated. It didn't sink in then that the schools who were on the ball enough to pick up on this new program in its first year were going to be the most innovative and the best organized anyway.

Some of the others in the program were having not-so-happy experiences. But for the most part it was a lack of organization and not lack of enthusiasm. Probably Heather Miller was having the most exhausting experiences. She had a few one week jobs, but most of hers were the one- and two-day jobs. When she and Randall Ackley were hired to cover the state there was no way to know that her part of the state would require about twice as much attention as his part. As a result she was obviously going to need some help to get all the schools covered before the school year ended.

Dr. Good called me and wanted to know if I'd be interested in some of the one- and two-day jobs. Yes, of course I would. Why not, it was all as easy as ripping up Rod McKuen! Well, the reasons why I shouldn't have were many. It involved more travel and more staying in motels alone and more hassle and more everything. Mainly, these days were not planned a tenth as well as the whole week jobs.

It was good that my first jobs had given me some experience and confidence, because some day jobs were real "trips." Many times I'd arrive and was thrown into whatever classes seemed to be available at the time. Some of the time the principal was not aware that some teacher had asked for a poet to come and I'd spend the first hour explaining why I was there in the first place. In one office, I got a shock when I dropped by on my way out to pick up my check. They thought I was working free. Tactful as I thought I was being, somehow it got to be my fault that I was supposed to be paid. The teacher who got me there in the first place was summoned and I was allowed to leave with the promise of payment which I did later get.

Another day I got to a school and literally nobody knew why I was there. It turned out that the teacher who was responsible for my being there was home with the flu and had forgotten to tell her substitute what the deal was. I taught my four classes, but as I recall one of them was a chorus class, one was a shop class, one was a "low class" with ten boys, and the last one was a journalism class who sat there and wondered not too politely who in the hell I was for an hour as I tried to explain why meter and rhyme aren't very important any more.

It finally got to be funny and my husband and I would have all sorts of crazy guessing games about what could happen next. But nobody could come up with anything stranger than the truth. Like the mountain school I arrived at one morning to find the students staging a walkout. Did they hate poetry that much? No, they hated the new regulations about credits and hours to graduate. It took two hours to settle and by that time half of my classes had been expelled. I finally got a group together in the library where I spent another hour trying to wrest a slide from the slide projector since I had decided to use slides to give them something to think about and write about. The last two hours of the day I spent with a mildly interested group of students being constantly interrupted with news from the front.

The one- and two-day jobs were sometimes rewarding, but were for the most part a drain on everyone concerned. A couple of schools I went to still send me school booklets and I know that my going there really didn't make that much difference even though they are nice enough to try to acknowledge that, for one or two days three years ago, I was in their school. These schools have such strong teaching leadership they would be precisely in the same spot whether I had come or not.

In the meantime things were going smoothly in the majority of the other schools. Most of the teaching poets were happy and so were the schools. Personally I was relieved and terribly excited to know I could go into a classroom and turn kids on to poetry. They actually wrote and they liked me and the teachers warmed up and thought I was doing something good. I mean how heady can life get! Looking back I realize that the poetry I got from the elementary students wasn't as good as what I get now, but the high school pieces were about the same. Many things account for that. In the elementary schools, experience and study on my part have corrected some of the sameness and exercise type stuff that I got that first year. In the high schools I was always on my own and in a lot of ways I was closer to doing with them what needed to be done. And everything didn't need translation. But then, that year, I was doing what I thought was a great job. We were all so enthusiastic and everyone was so appreciative. I mean here we had come and created a poem in a vast cultural wasteland and even the teachers liked us.

Toward the end of the program for that year, around April, I had a call from Jim Hall and Mel Good to come down to the State Department of Public Instruction to talk. As we talked, the gist of their problems rose to the surface. They owed the National Endowment an evaluation and a collection of student work. Competent as Mel Good was, all that music background of his wasn't coming in very handy in the poetry field. In short, he couldn't make heads or tails of the evaluations from the poets, not having ever worked in the classroom in this field, and furthermore, according to him, he couldn't tell the poems from the evaluations! He was relieved even to consider that someone would come in and take it off his hands and head.

What it boiled down to was that I was hired to come in and wrap up the first year, write the overall evaluation, collect the other evaluations from participating poets, edit a student anthology, and make some suggestions about the way the program should be run the following year. All this with the understanding that if an outside administrator was hired for the next year that I would get the job. I started the next week, which was the first week in May, which was far too late, but had to do.

I knew I was in trouble when I had a drawerful of papers stacked on my desk, none of which seemed to match. We had poems from only a few of the schools and not even that many evaluations. Work had to be done fast because (1) the schools were due to close, and (2) the publisher doing the anthology could only promise us the anthology by October if we got it to them by the end of June.

We sent a polite note to poets, schools, administrators, saying we "have noticed" that such and such was not in our files. That got us about a third of what we needed. Then I sent desperate pleas and began to call the schools. That netted us a bit more. Finally blood, anguish, and threats (you wouldn't want us to put your name in the front and then not print any poems, like your kids didn't write any, would you?) got me the rest.

Then, of course, there was another minor problem. I had never in my whole life edited or published anything. I went up to the publications department and found Jim Jackman, their publications expert, and finally found out what to do. Then I made a decision I would probably never have made if I'd had a shred of sanity left. I decided that my time was so limited that I would choose the poems for the anthology myself. I consider it a miracle that nobody ever complained. Actually, I looked so wild at the time anyone would be afraid to complain.

At this point, I was compiling the evaluations as they came in and choosing the poems as they appeared in the mail. I'd take the poems to the typist, Notie Brents, an executive secretary in another building, who because of her love of poetry and belief in the program had agreed to type the poems.

There was nobody in our office who had the time to do the meticulous job that needed to be done. Anyway, as Notie was typing, I'd come over and correct and she'd type again and we'd put them in a pile and hope that when the time came there'd be enough to make a book.

There were all sorts of difficulties. Some schools had only a few poems because they didn't know they were supposed to save them and the poets didn't either. Some schools had a lot of poems that were absolutely dreadful and some schools had a lot of poems that were terrific. Each category brought its own problems. I was trying with each decision to be fair to everybody including the program itself. In addition, it appeared that we had all used the same book and some had even used it in the high schools.

So we had more wishes, lies, dreams, colors, sounds, and comparisons than even Kenneth Koch. Enough to make me yet turn green when someone says "red is like a rose." I guess reading all those thousands of poems that year and then again the next was the main factor in my search for "something different" or for newer methods of getting better actual real live poetry. How does one "bring 'em back alive?"

I finally decided to group the ones that demanded grouping, put the humorous ones together, and let all the rest that had that something extra to offer make up the last half of the book. The book had to be pasted up twice, once with the typewritten poems on pages set to size, and once on real pages once the galleys were ready. We used a slide rule to figure out how much typed material would fit on what size paper once it was set into typeset. At last it was finished for the first time and off to the printers.

In the meantime, as much material as possible had been sent to the National Endowment for the evaluation. There was a folder each of teacher evaluations, poet evaluations, resumes of the program, examples of student work from each school, and a Xeroxed copy of the pasted-up anthology.

During the summer we must have corrected ten galley proofs of

And All I Have for Tenderness Is Words. The printers couldn't understand why I was so insistent about spacing and punctuation and line breaks and I couldn't understand why they continued to make the same mistakes no matter how many times I marked them. There came a time when I had to make some disgruntled compromises in order to have the first copies by fall. Even then it was November before I had the first books in my hands, but very satisfied hands they were.

It turned out that the anthology was good that year, but as tentative in a number of ways as our moving into the schools. It did show that there was talent out there and that our poets had worked with a lot of enthusiasm to get the creative process flowing. The anthology was more sophisticated the next year and actually much better, but never more exciting than the first year's to the ones of us who were there.

Another tangible productive result of the program was the writing and printing of a small book on methods by Charleen Whisnant and Jo Hassett. Charleen was one of the poets in the program and Jo was one of the teachers she worked with. Together they wrote *Poetry Power* which we paid for, the writing and printing. It was a collection of ideas mostly from the two of them, but which did include some ways of teaching from some of the other poets in the program. Later they rewrote it and updated it a bit and Doubleday brought it out under the title of *Word Magic.*

With the anthology off to the printers, and the evaluation material off to National Endowment, I was ready to make some proposals to Jim Hall for the coming year. We estimated how much money we would have if the financial creek in D.C. didn't dry up and I took a look at the evaluations that had come in. I made notes and added my own opinions.

We had had poets in twenty-nine schools for a week residency and three of us had done one- or two-day residencies in approximately fifty other schools. My feeling was that the week long jobs were going fairly well, but that the one- and two-day jobs left a lot to be desired. I voted to eliminate them and to concentrate on more of the week long jobs. We knew that in a lot of states there was more concentration in one or two schools with one or two poets. I discussed this with Jim Hall, as well as going back to the same schools this next year with the same poet or a different one to do some follow-up to the year before. I was in favor of this latter move but Jim was not. He had his reasons and they were good. He felt that there were so many schools that still had had no exposure to any of the cultural arts that we could not allow ourselves the luxury of follow-ups just yet. His feeling was, let's see how much of the state we can cover this year and then next year we can begin to fill in the holes and gaps that are left. His hope was that as each school or system became more aware of the arts through the smattering they received the more willing they would be to try something on a local level.

Probably the best way of getting a feel for the program as it went that first year, and the way I used to determine how things should go the next year, is to take a look at parts of the evaluative comments the various poets made about the program. I will not include at this time any of the teaching methods, but rather go on to comments on general feelings and ideas about organization.

The following are comments taken from the evaluation of Heather Miller, the poet who did the most of any of the poets that first year, since she did week long jobs and a considerable number of the one- and two-day jobs.

". . . Screening was done prior to my arrival in some schools. Students were asked to volunteer for the writing class, or students were required to submit poems to be judged by the regular teachers before being admitted to the class. I have mixed feelings about screening. While you may get a concerted group, one really interested in writing, you may also discourage other students who might wish to try their hand at it. Others may simply wish to get out of regular English classes. I can hardly blame them, but such tactics still give the project a black-eye.

"To my knowledge, however, screening was done only in the high schools, never in the elementary schools. . . .

"I would suggest that the scheduling arrangements be handled by the Department of Public Instruction directly with the English or Language Arts teachers involved, rather than through the Superintendents, Principals, Project Directors, Cultural Coordinators, and Assistants. It was my experience that these persons often failed to pass on the Department's guidelines to the teachers, resulting in great confusion, especially where the one- or two-day visits were involved.

"In cases where the guidelines were not passed on to the proper teachers or even discussed, the teachers and students had no idea what my visit was to accomplish or how it was to be conducted. As a result, students were often packed, one-hundred strong, into auditoriums or gymnasiums, primed for a lecture-performance rather than a writing class. When this happened, I attempted to divide the students into smaller groups giving each group a different writing assignment, then pooling all the results for a mass class-discussion.''

Heather Miller ended up by making the same suggestion I had made which was to eliminate the one- and two-day jobs and to make the week jobs perfectly clear to everyone involved. The majority of her report was on teaching methods and working with the kids in the classrooms.

Betty Adcock suggested that "the teachers involved should have a better understanding of what's coming.'' Also, "I think it might be appropriate to inform the schools that this program is not set up only for 'gifted and talented' or 'high achieving' classes. In some schools I took some extra classes in order to be able to teach students who were not necessarily 'honor-roll' material. Of course it's a pleasure to work with the higher classes, but I gained something, and I hope the students did, by sessions with some of the less-motivated. . . .''

Jean McCamy did a lot of question and answer sessions with her kids with good results. She worked on the theory that the better the kids know you the better they'll write for you. The following comes from her evaluation.

"There were some questions I could depend on from every group: What inspires you to write? Who's your favorite poet? What is poetry? How did you get started as a poet? Have you always written poetry? There were always a few students who said, 'I don't like poetry.' (But they always turned out to be the ones who had never come in contact with anything except textbook poetry.) And, of course, there were a few students who slept through the discussion, but they did it politely.

"In addition to the standard questions, I got a wide variety of interesting and unexpected queries: How do you feel about death? Do you agree with Poe's philosophy of poetry? As a creative person do you think you are more liberal with your children? Which comes first —your family or your writing? Why is the poetry that is supposed to be so good so hard to understand? Is Rod McKuen sacrificing quality for quantity? Are you concerned about what people will think of your poetry after you're dead?''

Guy Owen made the following administrative suggestions. The classes should be limited to four a day at most. There should be a mimeographed evaluation sheet for everyone. Teachers should stay in the classroom while classes are going on. Poets should have the same kids all five days.

Of course, most of the above was spelled out for the schools and teachers involved but evidently not well enough. There were many evaluations from other poets that mentioned exactly the same things. Evidently schools were "stacking" classes, and teachers were drifting off to lounges for "just a minute" and never coming back. Certainly these were points that needed clarification.

The factors that Sally Buckner found most positive were:

"1. Having a large attractive, sunny room all my own, appropriately 'decorated' with art and a bulletin board display on poetry;

"2. the faculty's cooperative attitude;

"3. the willingness of secretaries, librarian, faculty, and students to help in getting materials, equipment, etc."

She had the following suggestions to make to improve the program:

"1. A brief meeting early in the week (probably Monday) with the English teachers to give poet and teachers insight into what each is emphasizing;

"2. another meeting at the end of the week so teachers can decide how best to follow up on the poet's visit, and so poet can evaluate how his work has meshed (or not meshed) with the school's expectations;

"3. more preparation for the poet's visit by way of duplicating some of his work and distributing it among interested students;

"4. scheduling as few outside distractions as possible. This includes schoolwide and class activities of a special nature."

Randall Ackley felt that the students should be allowed to evaluate the program also, in addition to the poet and the teachers. Sometimes they see things that the teachers don't. He felt this was particularly important in the schools such as some of us observed where the teachers turned to grading papers while the poet was there and "got back to business" when he left. It would not take a scholar to realize that if the poetry program was that unimportant to the teachers and their overall education concept then they sure weren't going to be able to (or wouldn't) evaluate it too well. He also felt that it would increase the efficiency of the program to have a poet as consultant, "either administering the program or advising the administrator on choosing poets, matching schools and poets."

Maria Ingram found that one of her schools thought she'd be lecturing on terminology, types, giving readings, and teaching appreciation six hours a day. She suggested that this could have been avoided by the Department of Public Instruction making the terms of the visit more explicit to the schools. Of course, these things were al-

29

luded to, but it was quickly apparent that the terms would indeed have to be spelled out if something of this nature took place. Also, it appeared that she was expected to and did, out of a wish not to rock the boat the first times out, teach five classes a day in one of her schools and six in another. Fortunately, Ms. Ingram's good nature, charm and grace carried her through to still be able to remark, "I loved it!" And the administrator of the school passed on this delightful comment about Ms. Ingram. "As one student confided, 'I have never met anybody I've been more impressed with, and I've been to South Carolina and Georgia!' "

Emily Wilson made the following suggestions about the program. "It would be helpful if the poet knew something about what kind of teaching of poetry was being done with the children already and if the teachers had some advance discussion of what the poet wanted to do. I definitely think the poet needs to be at the school at least for a week and meet with the same students each school day. It is completely unrealistic to assume that the poet will conduct discussions with teachers and parents and/or give a public reading and/or write his own poetry during a week that includes the kind of workload we undertook. Some suggestions need to be made to the schools about the publication of the children's poems—how they should go about it, the need to do it, etc. (This is apart from whatever use the state intends to make of the submitted poems.)

"It's easy for the mechanics (typing, etc.) to get dumped on the poet. During the week school staff members should talk with the poet and help evaluate what is going on. Beyond a casual approach to conduct, the poet is not responsible for maintaining discipline in the classroom; the poet should have teachers' suggestions about what kind of order they think is required, and when disorder goes beyond set limits, the teacher should deal with the offenders. If the poet does not mind any amount of disorder, he should get the teacher's consent and then take responsibility for the class. One general comment: as a rule schools try to get the poet to meet too many students, crowding in large classes for 'exposure' to a poet. They should be encouraged to make bigger gains with smaller numbers."

Suzanne Newton suggested some of the same things already mentioned, zeroing in again on "reaching an understanding with the classroom teachers about what role they can best play in the program in the matter of carrying out the ideas when the poet had gone." She also suggested that we "make an all-out effort to find collections of contemporary poetry that children can read, and make these available both to the school libraries and to the poets." She was interested in providing a time and place for those working in the program to get together and share ideas.

Many of the poets mentioned the fact that they wished they could use more films, but didn't have access to them. The North Carolina State Library Film Service was not available to the schools at that time and could only be used in libraries for community use.

Also, many complained about the samples of student work. Some had the whole thing dumped in their laps, to read, comment on, correct, type, send in, fix for publication in the school, etc. The ones who were lucky enough to leave it all up to the teachers and secretaries found that the selection of poems was miserable and some of the best, imaginative poems found their way into the trash instead of the anthology. Many were moaning to me at anthology time or when the schools sent them their copy of the school anthology, "My poems, all those gorgeous poems. What happened to them?"

There were many ideas pushed back and forth about the content of the classes. Among them was one by Dr. Paul Baker Newman: "I had the best results when the program was voluntary. The students seem to work harder and to produce more and better work. I would recommend that attendance at next year's programs be made voluntary, insofar as possible."

Some of the poets wanted classes of kids where the mix would be low to high achievers, some wanted just high, some swore they never wanted another creative writing class as long as *they* had to teach it. This appeared to be more of a personal preference than anything else we encountered in the evaluations. Also, everyone had his or her favorite age group to teach.

There were a number of comments about liking a room to stay in all week so the students could find you if they wanted some individual attention. And it helped to have a blackboard and some place to set up the record player and slide projector or overhead projector if needed. And it really helped to have all of these there and working when you needed them.

Needless to say, the ideas expressed in the evaluations would shape the next year's program. The teachers sent pretty stock letters of evaluation expressing their appreciation for the wonderful experience and all good and nice, and sugar and spice stuff. Not much help there, which was frustrating, because you knew they had plenty to say, just weren't sure how honest they could be and not have it reflect on them. The next year we would have to make up a question sheet that would make them tell the things we needed to know.

Everything seemed to be tied up for the year at that point. The anthology was off to the printer, the evaluation was off to the National Endowment, notes had been made for next year, we had the poets' evaluations to study, and my proposal was in Jim Hall's hands. With this I decided to take a break. My children had been out of school for three weeks and still no mother in sight. Hall said they did want me to coordinate the program for the next year and we made our arrangements for me to be back in August with my ideas ready to go. We agreed on a price which didn't include what I finally added, which was my body and soul and everything in between, and the first year of North Carolina's Poetry-in-the-Schools was over.

Chapter 2

GETTING IT TOGETHER

"To live is to defend a form."
—Anton Webern

During the summer, I had many questions about the program to ponder on and wonder about and come up with some answers. One of them involved my own personal concerns about teaching and teaching methods. I also wanted to find as much material as possible about this animal, teaching writing.

Also, I needed anthologies to take into the schools to inspire the librarians to order some contemporary poetry. Many of them had simply given up the fight with parents and school boards years ago about putting an anthology of new poetry in the library. There was sure to be a "hell" or "damn" or worse in every last one and everyone knows that our innocent children can't be exposed to that sort of rot in the school building proper. Anyone who has been in the halls of a junior high school during break would realize that those innocent ears can't stand the possibility of being tainted by one of those awful words in the poetry anthologies. I mean, really! However, such blindness does exist in parents, and librarians do have to take the guff when there is any and you really wind up not being able to blame them for protecting themselves with the security of Frost and Sandburg. If there does happen to be a bad word in one of their poems, at least it's an articulate and classic bad word. But, the fact remained that there were almost no contemporary anthologies on the shelves for the kids who were interested by the time the poet-teachers left. Hopefully when our anthology came out the schools would order it and that would help some. Still, the kids needed to know what the outside world of poets was writing. To most it was a revelation in the classroom when you read them some of the contemporary work. It was the kind of thing they could understand and maybe even write something like.

But, to get back to the teaching. I figured if I followed up on my needs they would more than likely be about what the other poets in the program needed also and I could share with them and that would help the program as well as me. Of course, I had ordered a number of books through the spring and had been made aware of others when the evaluations came in from the other poets in the program. Still, I wanted to know what else had been written about the poetry program specifically and what other states were doing and how did other people go about it.

Through the few things that had come in to our Arts Council and been forwarded to me, I realized that just about everyone else around and about the country was as in the dark as we were. In other words, there was a lot of groping around going on. Reading the anthologies from other states, we thought we were creeping along better than most.

Sometime during the summer, I found out about Teachers & Writers Collaborative and ordered everything they had as well as started a subscription to their *Newsletter*. It was definitely the most productive thing I had done. It was like somebody had said, "Let there be information," and there was. I read and underlined and in general lapped up every word. When *The Whole Word Catalogue* arrived, I knew what "the promised land" was all about. From it I also learned about Ron Padgett's compilation, "The Book of Methods," which I ordered and loved. Also about the California magazine, *The Big Rock Candy Mountain,* which was talking about things nobody had even dreamed of yet on the east coast. (Now sadly gone, but some back issues exist for buying, see Bibliography.)

All of this was back before the time of *A Directory of American Poets* and the Poets-in-Schools supplement of *American Poetry Review.* In fact, it was before the time when most people even knew what was going on except Koch and the few mentioned above. Yet, they gave me ammunition. I felt good about meeting my teaching needs finally. I figured that with all that information to pass on to the poets working in the program, plus the list of materials they had suggested in their evaluations from the first year, plus some of the books I had ordered that were worthwhile, I had enough for all of us to work with and bounce-off of in the classroom for the next year.

The second concern for the summer was not so easily resolved. It was administratively directed. I read all the evaluations and comments of everyone involved in the program the previous year and took notes. The program had been funded again with almost twice the money of the previous year, so I had a big program on my hands. What was the best way to run it and the most clear and the most efficient. By August, after many drafts and redrafts and lists and more lists and forms and reforms, I thought I had most of the answers. (By the next August, I had all questions again but that's another book.)

I had made two big decisions upon which all the program would hinge and sway. One was that I'd try to have the poets in the schools by November and out by the end of April (the previous year, it had been January and end of May). This would facilitate the evaluative situation and help get the anthology show on the road. The second was that we would definitely give up the one- and two-day jobs and concentrate on the one week. All three of us who did the day jobs had stated that they were not the best way to work. They were expensive and trouble and smacked of "entertaining the troops." The three ring circus which swirled around the question, "What's he/she doing here?" wasn't the right arena for this program.

Putting aside money for the next anthology, setting up approximate expense account money, conference money, and miscellaneous funds, I figured I had enough money to put poets in schools for 62 weeks. At that time, the North Carolina Arts Council folks and my boss in the Cultural Arts Division of the State Department wanted to cover the state with as many poets as possible in as many school systems as possible. So I decided to put a poet for a week residency in 62 separate schools. (Later we added a few more.)

Once that was decided, it remained to wrestle the beast until it took some sort of form. It was obvious, to me at least, that very stringent rules and regulations would have to be established for the whole program to function. There would have to be common ground on which we could all do our thing; freedom, but within a certain framework. It was going to have to be a tightly run program administratively, but still allowing each poet and each school to establish some of their own rules to retain their originality and serve their purposes. However, some things would have to be constant. Somehow, I would have to distinguish between them and then enforce them.

It might be of interest to mention at this time the physical makeup of the state of North Carolina and something in general about the student bodies (collectively and individually) for whom we were carrying out our mission.

North Carolina is a long narrow state, over four hundred miles long from east to west and about one hundred and eighty miles wide from north to south. It starts out on the west, deep in the heart of the Appalachian Mountains, and ends up with its right end sliding into the Atlantic Ocean. The Coastal and Mountain regions are considered to be deprived in the areas of the arts, big business, and education. They have, however, grand natural resources, among which is the scenery, which is brilliant, yet calm and soul satisfying. The Piedmont area is the busiest, with industry growing more every year, lots of trees and grass going as it comes, with numerous art groups, much culture developing.

The area in which a poet taught would affect his or her approach. Teaching a group of kids in a remote Appalachian community, some of whom may not have ever seen a movie, and teaching a group in a swinging, culture-hip area like Charlotte were going to be two different affairs.

The North Carolina Arts Council was very busy at that time with a staff of five trying to spread knowledge of the arts across the state. They, like the Cultural Arts Division, were laying much groundwork for the network of the arts as it exists in the state today. It is much easier to go into any community and school with artistic endeavors now than it was then.

The racial issue was then, and is to a certain degree now, very much alive, with the Mountain and Coastal regions getting the blame for most of the tension while the Piedmont, just as guilty, hides it better under an exceptionally thin veneer of brotherhood, and intellectualism. When the poetry program started we were in the first stages of massive busing and in some of the schools we were in, it was their first year of real integration. There were great caution talks given to all of us about observing race relations in the different schools and taking care not to upset any apple carts. In some the tension is still great enough to have some bearing on how you would approach teaching "Black" poetry for instance. Most of it ringed about the junior and senior highs because the little ones fortunately didn't really think in black/white terms yet.

Needless to say, the poet or the person with any integrity wanted desperately to get to these students with good black poetry, to let them know that there were black poets and what they wrote spoke to their experience and that they, the students, could also write and speak of their feelings and life styles and even use the words they were comfortable with. But it was extremely hard. The librarians were over an even bigger barrel than usual in getting black poetry anthologies past the censors, because there were almost none that didn't ring with good street talk, an honest ring to be sure, but a ring that wasn't included in many textbooks with the usual copyright from six or seven years back. That problem fortunately has been solved somewhat with the advent of Black Studies courses.

The racial balance in most of the schools then was approximately 70-30, with the Piedmont black ratio higher and the others lower. In those communities where "Academies" had been started the black school population greatly outnumbered the white.

A poet going into a school this particular year had to know something about what was going on if possible. Were things tense, or not? How would the black and white students react to talking about protest poetry? Would they feel threatened if you even mentioned the problem that loomed over everybody? Would the poet feel threatened by the behavior problems that existed? There was more to going to a school than just appearing for a week and doing your thing. It was obvious to me that I would have to gauge my poets and my places and send people out to problem areas who had a bit more savvy about the education system and where it was at that time.

None of this is to indicate that the problems were anything like those encountered in some of the ghetto schools and inner city schools in other states. Nowhere in this state was there at that time anything approaching the likes of some of the situations of the big cities. Racial balance meant some tricky situations but balance was the key word. You might run into a few discipline problems, but no ghetto situations and no absolutely miserable running amuck classrooms. There were some minor problems, but no impossible ones, at least as far as the students were concerned.

Because of the situation, I felt we should make an effort to have as much of a heterogeneous grouping situation as possible. The first year the schools made up the classes. In some, the top four classes in English were chosen. In others the program was put into four classes that conveniently fitted the school's schedule. In others, the suggestions from the State Department were so blatantly abused that it was impossible for anyone to function. The poets needed to be protected and the schools needed their money's worth — within reason. But the major thing was that we needed to be sure the make-up of the classes reflected more of the intent of the program, which was not to cater to the top students in each school.

In addition there were emotional logistics to be considered. With as many schools as we were taking on we were going to need every able-bodied poet in the state to do the business we had drummed up for them. This meant keeping some of the poets happy all the time. The poets and the people in the schools were going to have to take a look at each other as human beings before they came into the school. If the poet went in with a long list of "this is what I will and will not do" and was met with a similar list from the teacher who was the liaison person in the school, the meeting was going to be doomed from the beginning. I felt that part of my job was going to be laying down the law and then holding everybody to it. In other words, let them get mad with me if necessary instead of each other. After all, I could sit in Raleigh and not have to work with the people in the school like the poet had to. It is awfully hard for a poet to be having dinner the first night in a town with the principal, teacher, and other involved parties and refuse to take that extra class. But I could sit on my rock in Raleigh and say no in a minute. I decided at that stage in my thinking that it would be a good idea for me to work out the schedule with the school and have them submit it two weeks in advance for approval.

I suppose the main decision I came to during the summer was that all the ins and outs of the program really needed to be set forth to the superintendents, principals, and teachers in charge before they decided they wanted the program and then they couldn't say they didn't know what was going to be required of them. The same thing went for the poets. They should know what was expected of them and then they could decide whether they wanted to do it or not. Once committed, either of them, it would be up to me to help them have a good week and watchdog those commitments. If at any time either party wasn't willing to play by the rules they could leave. We would have plenty of poets and schools waiting in the wings to take up any slack that occurred. In other words, for the program to have the freedom it needed in the classroom, somebody was going to have to be horsey as hell on the sidelines.

For the program to begin in the schools in November, a number of balls had to be set rolling in August. The schools would take the longest to decide and consider and reply so we started with letters to them. Jim Hall wrote a cover letter to all the superintendents of school systems and I wrote a letter to all the principals. Included in the letter were many of the ideas previously mentioned by the poets from the previous year. This initial letter was not the one with all the guidelines, but just general items to start the selection process. A school could realize that this program would be a bit of trouble and that the program should not be applied for unless the school was willing to offer at least minimum cooperation.

The following is a copy of the letter to the principals:

August 8, 1972

Dear Principal:

For the second year North Carolina will have a Poetry-in-the-Schools Program. Poets and writers of professional stature will go into schools for one week and work with selected groups of students. Their main goal will be to acquaint the students with the field of contemporary poetry and to work with them in writing their own poetry.

The program last year was one of the most successful ever launched by the State Department. Teachers, principals, superintendents, and other school personnel saw students at all academic levels excited, inspired, and writing one poem after another. The teaching poets got results they never dreamed of getting and were in turn inspired and rewarded. Most of these experienced poets will be back with the program this year. A student anthology is in preparation that will speak for the program better than any description.

Even though our program is expanded this year, only 60 schools can be chosen to have a teaching poet. Only the week long visit will be offered.

We want you to know exactly what your responsibility as a host school would be should you request and receive this program.

THE HOST SCHOOL WILL:

1. Pay the poet $100 at the close of the week. (The remaining stipend and travel and living expenses are paid by the project.)

2. Appoint a chairman for the project who will be able to attend an orientation with the poets in Raleigh in November. This person will work with the poet to get best results in your school setting.

3. Be prepared to operate your school for this week to bring about a productive program which uses, but does not abuse, the poet. Several plans will be offered. All include four hours of teaching a day plus a poetry reading and a faculty conference.

4. Provide such audio-visual equipment as needed.

5. Help the poet compile a booklet of student work and duplicate this material for participating students.

6. Send a written evaluation of the week, along with 5 copies of the student booklet to the Department of Public Instruction after the poet leaves.

If you are interested, send a letter of application to me, incuding the time of year you would like the visit, and the name of the person in your school who will be chairman of the project so we can send communication directly to that person in the future.

Since the program will begin in November this year, time is at a premium. Our closing date for accepting applications will be October 1. This gives all school systems six weeks to apply. Schools will be selected on a fair and random basis to be decided upon and a committee will be chosen for this purpose.

Because of the amazing results from last year's program we wish every school in North Carolina could have this opportunity. Maybe someday that will be possible. Until then, let me say that if your school is chosen, I will be looking forward to working with you in this exciting venture.

Sincerely,

(Mrs.) Ardis Kimzey
Poetry Coordinator
DIVISION OF CULTURAL ARTS
Department of Public Instruction

The most important things I wanted were the schools' requests and the names of the people in the schools with whom I could make the most progress with the program. I had a feeling which turned out to be right, that the most important people in the program next to the poets would be the contact people in each school. I felt so strongly about it that if a request came in from a school without that person's name I would keep the application on file in the order it arrived but I would write back to the school that we couldn't process the application until we had the contact person's name. I had already decided that the time to get tough about the rules was from the beginning.

Next, we had to have a meeting to ascertain which poets we would ask to be in the program. This was certainly problematic. Everybody wanted to work in the schools, and why not. The money was good, $250 a week, a real windfall, and a lot easier to buy food with than contributor's copies of obscure "little" magazines.

I met with Jim Hall and with the Arts Council people and we came up with a committee who could have selected the president and nobody would have questioned it. There were a couple of poets who knew other poets and who had worked in the program. There were some newspaper people who regularly reviewed poetry and who had written with some accuracy about the program. There were some top administrators in the cultural arts, and of course our personnel and the Arts Council personnel who were involved with the program in any way.

It had been pointed out to us by the article in the newspaper the previous year, "there aren't 20 poets in North Carolina." Whether we agreed with that or not we had seen some people who weren't great poets be great public relations people for the program and great teachers in the classroom. So the considerations had changed a little, in that nobody was worried about whether somebody was an established poet or not. What mattered was that they be practicing poets, actively writing, and able to function in the program with the kids and be able to get along with the people in the schools. After all, being an artist is one thing, but being a responsible artist in a community is sometimes another. Yet we wanted to take a few more chances than the year before, try some young poets, some who really needed the money to live on, for instance, or who were trying to piece together an existence while writing or attending graduate school. I called or wrote teachers in some of the schools with good creative writing departments and asked for their advice. I wanted to get input from numerous sources. It was the year to get as many poets as possible spread across the state.

As it turned out, after a day of meeting, we had decided to ask 42 poets to participate in our program. Of the 42 poets asked, 32 replied that they would be able to work in the program. Later it was necessary to add two more poets and we asked two who had come to our attention since the program started. In the end, we had 34 poets in the program who would go into the schools.

I wrote the poets a letter much like the one we sent the schools, telling in general what would be expected of them. I also sent an information sheet on which I put all the information we had found we needed to operate the program. In addition, they were to send a picture and some samples of their work which could later be sent to their school. It should be mentioned here that I color-coded each item. For instance, the information sheet was green. The poet evaluation yellow, the student one white, the materials list orange, and so on. The colors were tacky, as can be imagined, but it sure made life easier all year. I also had a tremendous file cabinet in which I had separate files not only for all the materials about the program, but also for each poet and for each school. It was extensive but easy to pull a single item from each file in a hurry. It also helped at evaluation time.

The following is the information sheet sent to the poets to fill out and return if they wanted to work in the program.

POETRY-IN-THE-SCHOOLS

Poet's Information Sheet

Mrs. Ardis Kimzey, Coordinator   Cultural Arts Division
Poetry-In-The-Schools   State Dept. of
Program   Public Instruction

NAME:_____ AGE: _____

ADDRESS: (Home) _____

　　　　　(Business) _____

TELEPHONE: (Home)_____(Business) _____

SOCIAL SECURITY NUMBER: _____

PERSONAL INFORMATION: (Such as where born, married, children, etc.)

PROFESSIONAL INFORMATION: (Degrees, education, awards, where published, etc. This can go on a separate sheet of paper if necessary.)

( ) I will be able to participate in program.

( ) I will not be able to participate in program.

I could work ____ weeks. I would like to work in _____

　　　　　　　　　　　　　　　　　　　　　　　　(list month)

Age student preferred:_____

Day of week best to attend orientation conference
in Raleigh: _____

Please indicate if you MUST work in a particular area:_____

_____

(list area)

What newspapers serve your area? _____

_____

What radio stations serve your area? _____

_____

Date: _____

Upstairs we had our own publicity department, which is one of the joys of running the program from the State Department. I carried them all of the information each time we did something and they sent it out. In addition, I also made use of my contacts in the State on some of the larger newspapers. I called and made personal contact and followed it up by sending the information on the program. It was a good time to have the work out because it helped some of the schools decide to have the program by the little extra bit of prodding by the press. The following is a sample of the news release in August.

Poetry in Schools Program Begins

Students in North Carolina schools will have an opportunity again this year to express their innermost thoughts in writing.

Poetry in the Schools has been renewed for the 1972-73 term and expanded to serve some 60 school communities. The program, which brings students, their teachers and some of the state's native published writers together for one-week periods of discussion and creative writing, operated in 28 schools last year.

State Superintendent of Public Instruction A. Craig Phillips announced the opening of this year's activities saying, "Last year's highly successful project enabled many students, some for the first time, to write down their thoughts with a sense of pride and accomplishment. Teachers and other school officials reported that they were delighted to find so many students interested in creative writing. Today's student, I believe, thinks important constructive thoughts. He contemplates good and evil, war and peace, air pollution and efforts to ward it off, and numerous other forces that he knows affect him now, or will before long."

The 42 poets invited to serve in this year's program were selected recently by a committee made up of Sam Ragan, secretary of the Department of Art, Culture and History; Ron Bayes, writer-in-residence, St. Andrews Presbyterian College, Laurinburg; Melvin Good, consultant in the N.C. Department of Public Instruction's Division of Cultural Art, and Jim Hall, director of the division; Betty Hodges, literary editor of the Durham Morning Herald; Ardis Kimzey, Raleigh poet and one of last year's writers-in-residence; Edgar Marston, executive director of the N.C. Arts Council, which cooperates in the design of the project; and Heather Ross Miller, Elizabethtown novelist and poet, who participated last year.

Ardis Kimzey, a book reviewer for The News and Observer, has been named coordinator of the 1972-73 program. She is employed part time in the state education agency's Division of Cultural Arts. In addition to other duties, she is preparing an anthology of the student writings produced as a result of last year's program. The publication will be distributed throughout the state and used this year in English and creative writing classes.

Mrs. Kimzey explained that the program will not be able to serve all the interested schools because of a shortage of funds. "Our 152 local school systems have until October 1," she said, "to apply for the services of a poet-in-residence, and to find their $100 share of financial support for the writer's honorarium and expenses. A matching grant from the U.S. Office of Education will supply the remainder of the funds necessary for those one-week visits to the schools."

The matching federal funds are coming to North Carolina this year through Title III (experimental education programs) of the Elementary and Secondary Education Act of 1965, which requires one local school system to distribute funds to the others involved in the program. The Raleigh City Schools have been named the grantee school unit and will distribute the money under the direction of Federal Projects Director Curtis Fleshman. Last year's federal funds were channeled through the National Endowment for the Arts and distributed through the North Carolina Arts Council.

Something worked because the schools were getting excited. The requests began to pour in. Before the year was over we had over a hundred requests for a poet. As the schools came in they were marked with a number to indicate the order of arrival. Also, the name of the county was put in the upper right hand corner.

In North Carolina there are many different ways of formulating a school system. Some cities, such as Raleigh, have their own school system with the county which surrounds it having its own system. Some of the systems incorporate the large cities or small towns and the counties around them into one large system. Then there are the areas where each little town and community has its own system with one or two schools in it.

Trying as we were to spread the program around the state with some degree of fairness, we had decided to work as nearly as possible with the county divisions instead of the schools' system division. We would count the large cities as counties. With 100 counties in the state and several large cities, it appeared that we would have some luck in this dividing, if we had other considerations as well.

We decided that we wouldn't go back into the same school we had the year before, for previously stated reasons. If more than one school applied from a county, we took the first one that applied from a system in that county that had not had a poet the year before. If the superintendent from a system applied for all the schools in his area and that also happened to encompass the whole county, and that system had not had a poet the year before, we wrote and told him that he could have two weeks, and to choose the two schools where he wanted them.

There were many considerations and, needless to say, I spent a lot of time with a state map laid off according to counties and a State Department directory laid off according to systems. I had the most ridiculous looking list that I consulted before I made any final decisions. I was trying to do it well so that if anybody came in foaming at the mouth about their school not being chosen, I could whip out all my information and beat them over the head with it. As it turned out, the whole affair was so complicated I probably would have gone stark raving mad even a week later trying to reconstruct why one school got a poet and another did not. However, at the time I did it I'm sure it was fair. And, as luck would have it, nobody arrived at my door in such a state anyway.

45

During September while I was waiting on the schools and poets to get themselves together, I was getting myself together also. There was a conference to be arranged, and all the guidelines, evaluations, expense accounts, etc. to be written up and copied so that once the schools were chosen, I would be able to send material out with the letter telling them they were having a poet.

In the meantime, the poet information was also coming back in. By the time I got my list of schools finished, I had a list of poets to work in them, with their preferences as far as time of year, areas, age of students, and number of weeks listed on a long sheet of paper.

Putting the schools with the poets was supposed to be easy with all the information I had, and in a way most of it was. If a poet wanted to work with only high school students and could only go during a particular week, but would be willing to go anywhere (most poets were willing to travel throughout the State), then I simply matched up that poet with a high school who wanted a poet during the month mentioned. Again as luck would have it, our ratio of elementary, junior high, and senior high schools worked out almost on the nose the way we wanted it with very little manipulation.

The compromise that had to be made most often concerned the time the school wanted a poet. Many of them wanted a poet at a time when I simply couldn't get anyone out to them. Then I ran the risk of putting the poet there during accreditation or Greek Week or some other school affair. So, I had to give the school the option to change if I assigned a poet to them at a time they didn't ask for. Given the program to run over again, I would have asked each school to xerox a copy of the school calendar and send it in with the application. Most schools did indicate important things like school holidays. They do vary from one system to another. But I hit it lucky most of the time with the dates and most of them were satisfactory. After I sent out the packages to them about the program, I gave them a week to change the date before I made up the schedules and master sheets.

All the while, I was trying to arrange the conference and get all the information anybody would need all year typed up and duplicated. At the same time, I was making a daily call of harassment, which became a daily obscene phone call to the printers, trying to shock, beg, borrow or steal the anthology off of their presses.

The requests from the schools, the matching, and the mailings all took place the first week in October. The conference was scheduled for November 3 and the first poets were due to go into the schools the second week in November. We were running so short of time that I stayed out of breath all of September and definitely all of October. I wanted that anthology in the worst way by conference time. I felt that it would give everybody a lift. It was finally ready about three days before the big day and as I held the first copy of *And All I Have For Tenderness Is Words* in my proud mother's hands, I really almost felt sentimental about the poetry program for the first time in months. This quickly vanished and was replaced by the usual normal feeling of panic that all those schools and all those poets were bound not to get along and the whole damn thing was going to come unglued at any moment due to some colossal stupid error. The errors were there as it turned out, but they were not as drastic as those in my tumbling nightmares.

I momentarily left my plans for the conference and turned to getting out massive mailings to the poets and to the schools. To the schools I sent:

1. A conference invitation.
2. A letter with their poet's name and the dates of the program in that school.
3. A set of guidelines for the visit.
4. General information about the program.
5. Evaluation forms for students, teachers and administrators.
6. Information sheets on the poet, including poems, and pictures when I had received them. (Some of the poets waited and sent in poems and pictures after the conference, since they are hard to get sometimes in a hurry. I made a note of which schools had not received pictures and poems and sent them on out as they arrived in the office.) The information, of course, included addresses and home and office telephone numbers in case the schools had to get in touch with the poets on their own.

The package (see Appendix A) went to the principal and contact person in each school; that is, it was addressed to both on the outside envelope. That way, I hoped the principal would read the information first and at least know a little of what was going on and then he would pass it on to the teacher in charge. Not included in the previous pages is the letter Jim Hall wrote to each superintendent telling him which school or schools were involved in the program. We were trying to be as informative as possible so nobody could pop up and complain that we had a program going on in his school or school system without his knowledge. People forget unless they get numerous reminders.

I tried to make the mailings as informal as possible. The conversational approach would at least give them something more personal than the forms, memos, and instructions they were accustomed to receiving, glancing at, and throwing in the trash. Also, many times they have been told deadlines, and exact procedures, and then nobody ever followed up on them. I had to make it pretty clear that this was going to be a closely watched program. I did, however, want to make minor statements when necessary about the "whys" of some of the rules.

The finances are a good example of this. The year before, the schools had been told to pay the fee due to the poets from the school at the end of the week. About half of the schools actually did this. In some cases it really did work a hardship on the poet. It is a bad feeling to plan to pay your motel bill with that money and have a school tell you on the last day that they are "so apologetic" but that the bills all have to be paid at a certain time of the month, or that the check hasn't cleared the central office, or the principal left the office for a conference and forgot to sign the check when he left, or the school board member who was to sign the check was in the Bahamas for three weeks (true story). I mean that all begins to get a bit old. The schools expect the poet to be prepared when he or she gets there and my feeling was that it was not too much to expect the school to give some thought to their obligations also.

If doing it again, I would not have the evaluation work in exactly the same way. The previous year we did not get enough and the year I ran the program we definitely got too much. It really is necessary to get some feedback from the students, but maybe from only a few. The evaluations I had done by each student in the program in each school and then duplicated so one set could go to National Endowment were mainly a waste of time and paper. The natural feedback that I had hoped for turned into a reflection of teacher attitudes. After all, the students "live" with the teachers before the poet comes and again when he or she leaves.

On the whole, the evaluations of the students were like those of the teachers the year before, totally inconclusive on the actual events. On the other side of the coin, the teacher evaluations were great in telling what really happened. The administrators were a lot like the kids, more enthusiastic than informative. I'll go into the evaluations in detail later. But pertaining to the guidelines, I would change this section of them. It was an unnecessary burden on the teachers and didn't reap us the results we thought we'd get.

Having a program chairman was among the best things we did. Without them the program wouldn't have had nearly the success it did. I became quite close to some of these dedicated people during the year as we worked with various problems and/or ideas. I still work with some of them in different areas. I found them to be teachers living their students' educations in every pore; informed, enthusiastic people with a driving need to do what was the best for their kids. Of course we had some lemons and that always made the job twice as hard.

I felt that the directions for the booklet were explicit, and no nonsense, and as it turned out, they worked. The poets liked the idea of suggesting poems for the booklet and liked the idea of taking Friday's work home. But they liked best of all the idea that at the time they sent back Friday's work, their hands were washed and through. Many of the poets were moving on to other schools or going back to jobs and it was necessary for them to be as thorough as possible when they left the school. On the poet responsibility sheet, it can be noted that the poet also had a chance to make suggestions about what poems in their schools' booklets should be in the state anthology.

About the audio-visual aids; it really was ridiculous not to have access to a slide projector that worked or an overhead that the students could actually read off of, or a record player that didn't make jazz flute sound like a whistling, wavering penguin. For the price the school was, and we were, paying the poets, it was silly for them to waste an hour wrestling equipment. Needless to say, teachers are faced with this situation almost full time and you can sure sympathize with them after a week of trying to find something that works, besides the educational T.V. set.

Regarding the selection of students, the teachers couldn't, and still can't, bear to leave students out of the program. I am in sympathy. However, when almost every poet from the year before complained that the masses were getting to them and that under no circumstances would they ever undertake more than thirty students at a time and that they had to see those thirty kids each day of the week they were there and that they absolutely couldn't survive more than four classes and still read all those poems every day and night and decide whether what they planned for the next day was going to be the best thing . . . well, you have to take their word for it. Also, I'd done enough of it and was going to teach in the program myself and it was time for playing the game of "protecting the poet."

I gathered from my experiences and the evaluations I received later, at the end of the year, that most of the coordinating teachers simply didn't have enough stamina to get the teachers together before the poet arrived and a lot of the teachers still didn't know about the poet until arrival. Most did, however, plan a meeting and/or workshop with the poet and teachers together the first day as suggested. This seemed to engender good will, or set the teachers' teeth, according to how it went. But teaching the teachers didn't work. They are tired or not interested or indifferent. It would have been better to have them come to central locations, getting the day off from teaching and coming to it fresh, instead of at the end of a long teaching day. And the general attitude became: Wasn't the poet hired to do all that and why are we being told about it? In other words, I would take the teacher workshops and put them in another context for them to work better.

For the most part the location thing worked out well. There was always a teacher willing to give up his or her room for the week or there was a band room or choral room or art lab or somewhere that could be used for the poet to hang his or her hat. Mostly, a teacher gave up his or her room for the poet and went elsewhere for the week. Some of the schools found this to be a difficult thing to do, to ask someone to give up his or her room for a week and teach in the gym or some other likely place. I never could understand this being such a problem, but the schools made so much over it that I had to listen and believe that it was a problem. However, I also believe that it is a necessity for the student to know where the poet is located. From the poet's point of view, it is disorienting to walk into the building, seeing it for the first time, and not even to know where to go to the bathroom or get a cup of coffee. Having a room to steer from all week, especially in some of the huge schools we were in, was essential for one's balance.

What I watched more carefully than anything else were the schedules I requested the school to send me and the poet three weeks in advance of the poet's visit. I honestly believe that it was the single most important item that led to the well-being of the visit, to have all of that thrashed out and decided upon in advance. After the dates of visits were solidified, I went back, two weeks in advance of the poet's projected arrival at the school, and made a list according to schools of exactly when the schedule should arrive in my office. You will notice that that gave them a week's grace according to the guidelines. If the schedule wasn't in, I'd send out a memo that day to the school that I expected the schedule by return mail. If the schedule wasn't in in four days, I'd call the school, talk with the principal and have him or her have the coordinator call me right back with the schedule.

I only lost one school due to scheduling. The principal would not give up his notion that the poet should teach five classes of different students each day and I wouldn't budge and so we called it quits. I quickly substituted another school who was delighted to have the program just as it was. Often a poet would receive the schedule and I wouldn't. The poet might call in in a state of distress and emergency to declare the schedule ridiculous. Then I'd simply call the school, inform them that I hadn't received my copy of the schedule and would they send it on and when they did, I'd call the school back and get it worked out. A lot of the schools didn't like it much but officials with the State Department have some sway and certainly more than visiting poets. It worked out eventually, but I suppose this was one of the knottiest parts of the program. Of course, I expected it because the chief complaint of the poets from the year before was that they had been used and misused until they were exhausted at the end of the first day and vegetables by the end of the week.

So we were forewarned that the problem was still lurking out there and would have to be handled very firmly. Seeing it from the school's perspective means certainly having sympathy for them. Naturally, they want as much student coverage as possible for teaching and exposure purposes. Also, some schools were getting the P.T.A. to cover the expense. The P.T.A. raises money from the parents of all the children, not just the 120 we were proposing to reach. I imagine that most schools decide they would rather beard the lion in the State Department than in the local school area. But it seems that most of the schedules that were impossible came from two sources, teachers who didn't exactly understand the guidelines and teachers who chose to ignore them hoping that nobody would notice and that they could talk the poet into it on arrival. I imagine most of them really were surprised to find that we meant business about the items in the guidelines. As I mentioned earlier, I wasn't nearly so strict about the other items that had to be in. I did make a chart of them and mark stuff off as it came in. It's a lot different when you know someone is hovering over a chart with your school's name in it getting ready to flip if something isn't in on time, than thinking that the guidelines, after being sent out, had been forgotten.

The transportation problem was another one I thought should be simple enough, but a couple of the schools made a big deal about it. If a poet came in on the bus, and some did because they only had one car or none of the spouses work and need cars, etc., then I thought it would be a minor matter to have someone pick up the poets at the place they stayed and carry him or her to and from the school in the morning and at the end of the day. We allowed some taxi fares if necessary but I really did think it wouldn't be necessary. I'm afraid this got to

51

be a clash of wills at a couple of schools, you know the type, why should we have to carry the poet around and about. My feeling was why not, out of mere courtesy, if nothing else. Well, we're all so busy.

I wouldn't even print the reply to that which I had in my mind. It was all a bunch of bull and a lot of "to do" about nothing. There remains in my mind no valid reason why someone can't swing by a motel on their way to school and pick up a person standing there and take him or her to the school. And no reason why someone on their way home in the afternoon after school can't take a person back to a motel and leave him or her there. It's no big deal and one of the prime examples of pettiness that exists in the world.

I will have to say that in most all the cases where the poets arrived by bus, they were treated with the red carpet routine and taken wherever they wanted to go with utmost courtesy and hospitality and no questions asked and we're so glad to have you in our community for a week. It goes without saying that most people are going to blossom under that kind of attention and be ready to go into a school and do their best, with no reservations and no funny feelings about being wanted or not.

Most of the schools also had the poet out to eat the first night or at least came over or called in to make sure everything was going all right, whether the poet came by bus or car. It was reassuring to know that somebody actually knew you were in town and that all was ready for you the next morning. I always liked to ride around the town a bit and see the school so I could begin to get the feel of the community. This can be extremely important especially if you are teaching in a junior high or high school.

The publicity angle worked out in almost every school to a perfect T. The schools varied in the degree of how well or how extensively they carried out their publicity plans, but they all did something. It was interesting to note that the most unexpected comprehensive publicity took place in the smallest communities, involving the whole community often in the poet's visit although sometimes they only read about it in the paper.

All this time we were sending many news releases upstairs to the publicity department. The newspapers were doing a good job using the items we were sending them. When a school system was chosen to have a poet the local papers were hit from two directions, us and the local person in charge of the program. When the program was finished and certain kids' work had been chosen for the anthology, the papers would come out with something. Always they did an article or interview with the poet when he or she was actually in the area. As a result of all these different angles, the newspaper coverage was three times what it had been before. It came at a good time for the program because it gave us the publicity to provide the momentum in the communities that was later needed for some of them to formulate their own plans for a poetry program.

My favorite news article at the time was written by Rod Cockshutt, the same newsman who had blasted the program in the first place and who had dubbed us "Rent-a-Poet" the year before. The anthology had come out by this time and I carried him one in person. He wrote a delightful article called "Eating Crow on 'Rent-a-Poet,'" which is re-printed in Appendix C.

I mailed a sample copy of the anthology to all the newspapers in the state who reviewed books and they all printed something about it and it was all glowingly favorable. We also sent copies to school administrators, the principals, teachers, and to students who had poems in the anthology.

In the area of evaluations, the evaluations seemed to work better in a printed format than just asking the teacher to tell about how the program went in his or her school. For one thing, it told us exactly what we wanted to know about how well they really ran the program. It checked up a bit on how well the guidelines were followed and also checked up on the poet. We found out a lot more than we had the year before. It was as if some of the teachers rolled up their sleeves and said, "Now that you ask. ...". I have already made some comments about the student evaluations. If I ever do them again, I would probably not ask some of the ridiculous questions I asked then. During the second year I taught, and also when I got the evaluations, it was clear that the students weren't even going to work well with the language I used in the forms. Something that was interesting though were the choices of poems that poets read in the classroom that the kids remembered. Most of them either chose a poem that a classmate read or one of the poet's own. They were more impressed with the poems written by the people right there in the flesh, whether it was a classmate or the visiting poet.

At the same time I sent out the forms to the schools, I also sent out a large mailing to the poets. This included the following (see Appendix B):

1. A letter giving general information.
2. A form with assignments and dates, poetry chairman, address

of school.
3. A conference invitation (same as schools).
4. Guidelines for the poets to follow.
5. A copy of the school mailing of the guidelines for the schools and general information (so they could see what the schools had been told).
6. Poet's evaluation forms.
7. Two expense forms for each school assigned.
8. A sample expense form.
9. A materials list compiled from my materials and from the materials suggested by the other poets in the program the previous year.

Sending all this stuff off to the poets was a bit trickier than the mailing to the schools. For one thing, I knew most of them pretty well and they knew that I was, in general, easy to get along with, forgiving, and loved a good joke and lots of laughing. I ran the risk of making them think I was putting on airs, losing my mind, and/or really serious about this whole matter. The ones who wrote me back anything other than the information I asked have their letters duly filed at my house for future publication when they become famous, because they really are priceless. However, I was serious, and when most of them realized the scope of the job and how I really did have to have the things in on time and all that, they were most cooperative. In any case they all showed up at the conference and read poems and met dutifully with their people and for the most part did what they were supposed to do.

The time assignments were almost always okay and it seems that the ones that weren't were easily corrected before the conference. Later, as the year rolled on, many of them had to be changed for a number of reasons, but they were pat at the time we met at Raleigh.

The booklets from the individual schools were sent to the poets and to us with good results. Some of the poets did not mark their booklets and send them to us. However, I at least felt we had given them a chance to participate in the choosing of the poems for the state-wide anthology.

The expense account sheets were made up especially for the poetry program. The normal State Department expense sheets were so complicated that only the life-time employees could figure them out. We felt that surely some simpler way would work. And it did seem to work. As anyone can see (Appendix B), the money we allocated then for mileage and food and lodging would get you nowhere now. It was gracious plenty for mileage then; most people even made money on the mileage.

After the lodging, it was a little tough living on the food allowance that was left, but most ate a light breakfast, lunch at school, and had enough money left to have a decent supper. It was hard even then, however, to make ends meet if you were in a town with only one motel and it cost fifteen dollars a night to live there. On the whole though, everybody seemed to manage.

The evaluation forms worked out very well with the poets willing to take the time to do them. Needless to say, just as some of the schools and school chairpersons were not too hot, neither were some of the poets working in the program. This is not so much a criticism as a fact of life. If you're going to use that many poets, you're going to ring in some real losers, no matter how carefully they're chosen. But more about that later. The evaluations were extremely valuable in letting us know how well things were in the schools. They were less valuable in letting us know how well the poet carried out his assignment. You could be sure of one thing: if a poet filled out his evaluation sheet with two or three words to an answer then he wasn't much better prepared in the classroom. Oh the things that give one away.

It was now time to get on with the planning of the conference, getting the anthology out of the printers, fixing up some cross referencing schedules, getting some things ready to display at the conference, and getting some materials together to give the poets.

The place we had the conference was not exactly our first choice. The other auditoriums that the education people traditionally meet in were all in use because of a conference on exceptional children that was scheduled for the same day. I didn't even know about it until I started to find a place to hold our conference. I discovered from that experience that there was a master calendar somewhere in the building where one could find out such matters, but I found out a bit late. Everywhere else I tried either didn't have parking or food nearby or wanted terrible rent for the day.

Crabtree Valley was brand new at the time and had been the target of much environmental wrath. Many of the poets were less than happy to be meeting there because of that, but with a little begging and pleading they all appeared when the time came. As it turned out it was a perfect place. The lighting and speaker system and seating was workable and if it was less than cozy then I had to remember that I had almost three hundred people there.

This was the schedule and program we came up with for the conference.

POETRY IN THE SCHOOLS
NORTH CAROLINA
1972—73
*
Morning 10 AM—12:30

WELCOME............................. Sam Ragan, Secretary
Dept. of Art, Culture, and History

REMARKS.................................. Jim Hall, Director
Division of Cultural Arts, SDPI

QUESTIONS AND ANSWERS..................... Ardis Kimzey
Poetry Coordinator

PANEL "The Poet As Teacher"........... Moderator, Tom Walters
Maria Ingram
Heather Miller
Ross Talarico
Richard Williams

LUNCH BREAK
Afternoon 2:30—4:30

POETRY READINGS........................... Teaching poets

5:00—6:00

SOCIAL HOUR .... COMMUNITY HALL NORTH

The conference was apparently interesting to everybody concerned. I met for the first time some of the poets in the program. I liked them. I also was impressed with the teachers and administrators who were present. There was someone there from every school who was to have a poet. Sometimes they brought some students, sometimes there were several teachers or a principal and occasionally even a parent or two. Everybody from my department checked in at some point during the day, even the music and art people. Jim Hall was there all day, as was Mel Good. And of course Sam Ragan, Secretary of Cultural Resources, was there as moderator.

Before everybody came, the secretary and I set up two tables of display materials. One table had booklets from the previous year that had been turned in and that I thought were good examples of what could be done with student work. On another small table, we had copies of the anthology, *Tenderness,* which could be bought by putting the money in a shoebox, hoping all were honest.

On another table were all the books, articles, and magazines listed on the materials list I had sent the poets. That list also included books

56

of photographs, records, films, and other items handy to use in the classroom, which we did not have on display. I also had on that table extra copies of the materials list I had sent the poets. They were grabbed up fast by the teachers and I wished I had brought more. I told the teachers to ask the poet who came to their school for the list in order to make themselves a copy. This was one of many reasons I had made it up in the first place, to give the poets some additional information for suggestions to the teachers in workshops.

The poets were interested in seeing the books listed on the sheet. It is one thing to see a book listed as good. It is another to hold it in your hand and be able to leaf through it and see if it is good enough to order and buy.

The poets also had a package of their own given to them when they arrived. I bought folders with two pockets, one on each side as you opened it. In their package was a copy of the anthology from the year before, a copy of *The Whole Word Catalogue* (we had ordered one for each poet in the program), order blanks for getting the *Teachers & Writers Magazine,* and scheduling lists with everyone's addresses (see Appendix D), plus of course the schedule for the day.

During the question and answer period, I tried to be very informal to encourage informal questions and discussion. I thought people had pretty well covered most of the information that had been sent to them prior to the conference. The few questions that came up were explained most of the time by my calling on the poets in the audience who were waving their hands in the air eager to get everything straight before the program began.

The panel discussion gave everyone, teachers, and other poets alike, a feel for what some poet teachers are doing in the program. Here, again, there was a lot of give and take between the panelists and the teachers and the poets in the audience. I was extremely pleased with the whole interaction. Lunch was at the right time because, if there were still questions, the teachers and poets had an additional chance to get it straight with their contact in the school and/or poet. I expect that most of the schedule problems were worked out at that time. Everybody had an opportunity to have lunch with the one person or persons he would be working with later on. In many cases, the poets would meet with two or three teachers if they were going to many schools and through some of the contact teachers got a chance also to hear what was going to happen in other schools.

The afternoon poetry reading was probably more interesting to the other poets involved than to the teachers, but it did give them a chance to hear their poet. I had asked the poets to limit their reading to two poems each, since the year before it almost turned into an all-night marathon. I wanted the conference to end and the participants to go in to the social hour on time. I had the social because lots of people were heading home and needed something to eat before they left. It also gave everybody one last chance to get together to talk.

Chapter 3

MOVING OUT

"One teaches out of love; it's an impertinence, an imposition, in the end it's terrifying."

—Theodore Roethke

For about two months things went well. And I want to say now that I consider that the whole program went well. It is easier I think to tell about the pitfalls, because often you not only learn more from them but other people who are running other programs also learn from them. I would rather leave the overwhelming success of the program to be "understood" than to bore the everliving hell out of everybody by writing full time about how wonderful the whole thing is and the kids being adorable and creative to a fault and the teachers wholeheartedly running around with nothing on their minds but your program and how much they can learn from you and the administrators from the central office all over the schools wishing for a glimpse of the poet and reading all the work the kids do. And the news media setting up mobile units and taping the least word with all kinds of studio shots of the creative process happening right before your very eyes.

Talking about the "year's best fairy tales!" But I've seen reports like that, and yes, I'll admit, I've even written them, but everybody knows that the truth lies in a much tougher realm, one where some of these things happen some of the time, but never all in the same school or with the same poet, and that ten or more people are never in complete accord about anything nor for that matter are two. As a pure matter of fact, even I am not always in accord with myself about what's going on!

So with that off my ample chest, let's get back to my original thinking about how to talk about the way things really went. I'll try not to get ridiculous about the good parts, if you'll remember that they were there all the time that I'm going into detail about the bad parts in an effort to keep someone else at least from making the exact same mistakes.

I suppose the most irritating thing that took place those first few months before Christmas were the schedules not coming in on time and then having to hassle with the schools because of it. As I said earlier I had a chart with each school's name on it where I could check off the required items as they came in. Also I had a piece of paper with the date on it and what was supposed to be in that week. For instance, I knew that the week of March 10th I was supposed to receive a poet's schedule from one school, a poet's evaluation from another, the teacher and student evaluations from another school, and possibly a booklet of student work from another, or maybe the poet's marked copy of the booklet the school had sent him. It sounds complicated, but in fact it kept things from getting complicated and out of hand. I would have hated to get to the end of April for instance and gotten ten booklets and thirty poet evaluations in. I had the weeks scattered out so that wouldn't happen. It was also easier than it seemed because whenever I could, I had as many poets out as possible during the same week. I didn't do this in January and February because if the weather got bad, I didn't want to have twenty poets out caught in the middle of the week in eight inches of snow and no school going on. As it turned out, that was an exceptionally good idea.

A few matters came up in the beginning that were to be expected. Some had to do with transportation. We had made it clear to the poets that they could travel by bus if they chose and we would pick up the tab. Then came a request to rent a car. I figured and figured and talked it over with Jim Hall and we couldn't see any way to open that door for fear that it would take us a slide rule to ascertain differences in requests for car rental up against mileage payments. The other problem came about with the taxi requests from the poets who did take the bus to their destinations and who hated to ask someone to bother with taking them back and forth to the school. It could prove to be problematic if we okayed this and found that the poet was staying with friends and it was a twenty mile trip by taxi to the school (another true story).

Then, there was the question of staying with friends and paying them a little for the trouble of having a week-long guest. We decided that if the people would sign a voucher with a minimum amount per day on it that we would consider it. My feeling about this was two-sided.

If I were staying with friends it would more than likely be with such good friends that they wouldn't think of taking any money for it. On the other hand some of the poets stayed with teachers in the schools because they preferred that to staying in a motel. The teachers aren't really good friends yet and you would want to feel free to offer them something to stay there, and as far as the finances of the program are concerned it was sure cheaper than a motel. So the one rule I made about that was to be sure to have the poet check it all out thoroughly and carefully with the people they would be staying with and with me before they did anything.

From the beginning we also had a problem with getting the films I had assured the poets they could get. The films were in the North Carolina State Library and they had to change their policy even to allow us to get the films out of the library in town and take them into the schools. The films previously hadn't been available for showing in the public school system. There were many reasons for this, most of which I didn't understand and had to do with some of the conditions of the grant under which the films were originally bought. Another reason which didn't make much sense to me at the time and still doesn't was that they wanted to encourage the schools to have their own audio-visual equipment, which included film libraries. Well, anybody who has ever purchased a film at three or four hundred dollars can certainly understand why most schools are going to buy instructional films instead of those which are enrichment-oriented. In any case, we wrested the okay from the people over at the library only to find that in various cities where we went in all good faith, the films were unavailable for an assortment of different excuses. They were out of print, out of the office, out of the state, torn, wounded, had beriberi, you name it and we had it given to us. I don't want to imply any great conspiracy, but it all sure was aggravating and we wound up not using any more films than we had the year before.

I have been given to understand that since then things have gotten better. I know that the libraries are full time sending out the films to civic groups, library groups, and all such organizations, but the fact remains that they just aren't happy about them being in the schools.

As the poets began to finish their weeks we started our system of paying them. Occasionally I would have a question, or one would come in without a motel bill or other voucher attached and we would have to send it back out, but for the most part they were tidy and accurate. As they came in, I would add the totals from meals, lodging, and mileage together, add the stipend, write out the name, address, and Social Security number and we would forward it to the office upstairs so they could send the poet the money. We made a copy of this and attached it to the duplicate expense sheet we kept in the poet's file.

One of the poets kept forgetting, no matter what we kept telling him, that we had to have the motel bill from the motel he stayed in during the week, not just any old motel bill he had lying around. He was also the one who kept having car breakdowns. I'd be willing to bet we're the only poetry program in the nation who's been billed for an overhaul to a car transmission. (We didn't pay for it!) This poet was a friend of a friend and one who didn't work out too well. Be warned as I will forever be, always try to know who you're working with and where you can find them.

One poet was finally actually fired from the program. I don't want to go into it, except to document the fact that yes, despite the success, there are still problems, some of them severe enough to cause poets to be removed from the program. People think sometimes now when I run programs in cultural arts that I'm too cautious and too inbred about who is hired, but it's a good feeling to send out a poet and know that no matter what is waiting for that poet on the other end, he or she will come out of it, with respect for the program intact.

One of my hairiest moments as an administrator came as a result of the biggest comedy of errors we had all year. Even though the poets had been told that the poems they sent were going to be sent to the schools as examples of their work it somehow wasn't all that clear how they were going to be used and whether or not the kids would get to read them before the poets came. Many of the poets sent poems not suitable for the classroom or, as it turned out, for the teachers. This was not necessarily the poets' fault. Many were not in touch with the school systems and didn't know that the kids they saw swinging down most main streets were an example of their outside-the-school culture and not products of the classroom. In other words, they thought they would go into the schools and find them a new place, full of teachers in jeans and principals joking with the students during lunch break. All who thought this from afar were quickly brought up to date, or thrown back as it were, within ten minutes of arriving at their schools.

In any case the poems sent were honest examples of their work and were those they thought would be all right to send to the schools, at least for the teachers. Some of the poets, however, even thought that the poems were for my files and therefore anything would do. But the schools did like to see samples of the poets' work and they had been promised such, so I tried to go through those that were subject to arrest and put them to one side, sending only those in which I could find no evil words, suggestions or even ideas. Yes, they were few, but we found them, and of course, with the poets who had worked the year before there was no problem because they knew what to send. One of our young poets, a delightful and creative young man, had sent me his poems and in them I did detect some allusions that might possibly be taken the wrong way, especially in the mountain community I had him staked out in. They are our stronghold of moral indignation in this state, just as the east is our stronghold of social indignation. The young man I was sending up was sensitive and full of all the right kinds of feelings for the kids who needed tender loving patience when he discovered that they were barely reading, much less writing.

I carefully put all the questionable poems in one pile and all the "good" poems in another and very carefully mailed off the wrong poems. Well, the mail had no sooner hit the school than I had an emergency call from the superintendent. He was going on about how the principal had called him and said that that immoral poet was absolutely not coming into his school to ruin all those pure minds and, I suspect, told the superintendent where we could put our poet. This was too bad because the superintendent was a good young educator who hoped to modernize the school system. It was in fact he who had put in the request for the poet in the first place. We talked and talked and I apologized and we decided that he would call the principal back and talk with him and if he were still adamant, the superintendent was going to try to place the poet in another school in his system. If that didn't work I'd give him another poet entirely. Well, none of it worked, period. The system had been alerted by the first principal, a lion of moral vigilance, and not only were they not about to have that other poet, they weren't about to take a chance on one that might even prove worse! There was obviously nothing to do but make sad parting noises to the superintendent and make vague allusions to next year. I never did find out if they got anybody.

The poet was put in another school and I had to tell him why, but I don't think he really ever understood exactly what had happened. We had made a big to-do over choice of words and reading poems with no suspect words in them at the conference, so for the most part that was no problem throughout the year except in this one instance, which, ironically, I had caused. We had a few rumblings about a few poets and a few choice words, but nothing else this severe.

It used to be a difficult dilemma for me to tell poets to watch their language in their classes. I mean after all they were artists and creative people and why couldn't they say the words the students were using in the halls in the context of some very good poetry. There remains a controversy over this here and I often wonder if there are schools in some states that don't worry over such things. But now, and two years ago, in North Carolina, you had to watch your language or leave.

It got to be a matter of good sense where I was concerned. If I could find a poem that carried the message of what I wanted to say and it had objectionable words in it, then I'd simply find another poem. In other words, after all the grief I've gotten and seen other people get, both in the schools and in administrative situations, I have developed the school sensitivity that rides the rail right along with my teaching and creative sensitivity. My feeling has come to be that we are there to reach the kids and if we do something that makes the classroom situation tense or gets us kicked out or never asked back then we have served our own stubbornness and ego and not the kids. It does not hurt a poet to choose another word or another poem, but it hurts a lot of students if they are denied the program because of misuse of power in the classroom. I make it a rule to give my spiel to poets I'm about to hire and if they're not agreeable then I get someone else. Someone without the sensitivity to understand what I've said doesn't need to be with kids.

The funniest part of all this to people who know me best is that I'm sure they'd wonder how I could talk without a number of my favorite phrases or descriptive passages and words. I grew up around my father's mill and not only was my father a salty speaker, but so were all his friends and workers. You might say I learned all I know about certain parts of language at my father's knee. But I have usually had the good sense to know when I could be loose and when to curb my natural enthusiasm for profanity. Strangely enough it doesn't appear in my poetry either, which makes me a believer in oral tradition being more real than the written tradition.

As the winter progressed, many changes were necessary and some of the poets ran into some rather interesting problems which didn't have to do with the program but which caused repercussions and changes in the schedule. I mean, if a poet calls up and says he thinks he might have a nervous breakdown if he had to go out of town next week, you make other arrangements. There's nothing worse than having to send an ambulance from the local mental ward to pick up the visiting poet. And if another poet calls and says he's having a domestic crisis, you pay attention and either change his schedule or put someone else there. There would be no shootouts with irate spouses in the schools as long as I was running the program.

It really was interesting to find how open the writers were about their problems and situations. In probably any other operation if a person couldn't do something professional they would find some excuse or be evasive to get out of going for a week. In this case, I knew exactly where everybody was, and why, all the time, which made life interesting if nothing else, and there was always something else. Many times it put me in a divided situation. I could so easily "hear" what the poet was saying and I had complete sympathy, but I could see also what the problems were going to be administratively when I got to the office the next day. I think everything was resolved satisfactorily however and most things were only momentarily panic city. I will be forever grateful to those poets who were always ready to stand in for someone else gracefully and intelligently on almost literally twelve or twenty-four hour notice. There weren't many of those situations, but there were probably more of them than there would have been if I hadn't been a well-known friend to them, or if it hadn't been so widely known that I was flexible to the point of heart failure.

We all got into many wild situations. There were so many that I no longer remember all of them, but some do stand out in my mind.

In one of the schools I was in I stood at the window of the library and watched the entire police, highway patrol, fire department and sheriff's department arrive outside and run into the school. My kids couldn't see, fortunately, so I just kept on teaching. Then I saw lines of kids being herded out of the school. They forgot we were in the library. The librarian was in reach so I signaled her to go see what was up. There had been a bomb threat phoned in and the building was being evacuated, so I turned my students loose and told them to go outside and find their teachers and stay with them. It was close to the end of my class anyway and time for my lunch break.

I stayed out until my stomach decided there probably wasn't a bomb. Then I slipped back into the building and went to the teachers' lounge. There was one of the other teachers casually eating her lunch, so I went into the deserted lunchroom and went behind the counter, a major offense, dished up my lunch and went to join the other teacher. We had a delightful and uninterrupted lunch while everyone else was outside riding herd on the kids. I'm sure the lunchroom personnel were never aware of my terrible indiscretion and, after all, I did leave my money.

Another time to remember was when Sally Buckner was to go to a school and got up Sunday with a rapidly dwindling voice. She went and fought laryngitis all week, using a mike to talk and a very good sound system that the school had rigged up for her. She had the least discipline problems of all the poets as the kids strained for the words of wisdom whispered through the mike, and she also got some great work.

And I'll never forget Julie Suk traipsing around the countryside with almost a full nature museum with her. She worked in a nature museum at the time and had access to snakes and frogs and creepy crawlers, plus all kinds of ceremonial masks. So, when she checked into a motel, the maids were sometimes very reluctant to hose down the room. Fortunately and sadly, the snake died on the eve of departure and she had to make do with the other goodies. As she reported, she was getting along just fine until the frogs knocked over the crickets in the bathtub and they leaped all over her room singing cheerfully for the next three nights until she left. She never had the nerve to inquire back after their welfare.

Things like this were happening all over and I suspect that many more things happened that we never got wind of. We were sending such interesting people to such interesting people and schools and communities that the combinations were bound to make for an interesting time.

Some of the experiences I had during one of the weeks I went to a school were model examples of all the things that could possibly go wrong and the poet still be left upright. I had a student the previous year whom I had kept in touch with named Mandy Lyerly. Mandy was one of the most talented students I encountered during my teaching time and was continuing to write and send me poems and progress reports from time to time. She also dropped in on occasion to spend a night or visit for an afternoon when she was in the area. The year I ran the program we were already beginning to think in terms of helpers or apprentices from among talented students we had taught in the high schools who were then in colleges.

Mandy attended Salem College and there, as in many colleges around the country, was offered a mini-course in independent study during a four-week period in January. Mandy wanted to travel around with me and maybe someone else and work with us in the classroom, run errands, help praise the kids, and take on other helpful duties. Dubious as I was about weather conditions in January, I made my plans to take Mandy with me to the Outer Banks of North Carolina for a week where I was to teach at Kitty Hawk Elementary School. Then we were to return to Raleigh and she was to help me teach a free week in my kids' school, which had been promised for some time, and then on to Charlotte where she would work for a week with Maria Ingram, another poet in the program. The last week she was to spend writing up whatever was required for the college about what she had done.

I was excited to be going to Kitty Hawk and even more excited to have someone going with me. The Outer Banks remain one of our unspoiled resources in the state. Near Manteo, location of the famous disappearance, "The Lost Colony," you cross over a causeway and come onto the island which is comprised of Nags Head, Kitty Hawk and Duck. This is only one in a series of islands that makes up the Outer Banks, which runs parallel to our coastline, north and south. South of Nags Head is the island of Hatteras, better known as "The Graveyard of the Atlantic." South of that is the famous island of Ocracoke. reached only by an hour-long ferry ride.

The Kitty Hawk Memorial is visible from the beach along Nags Head and it was there that the Wright Brothers got the first plane aloft in the high Outer Banks winds. There was no question in my mind when the request came in that I personally would fill it. I felt it was my bonus for the year, to be going to such a quaint and grand place. At the time I had not realized that I would be going in January, but when Mandy and I put our heads together at the parcelling out time back in October, we both got excited about the prospect of staying at an ocean-front motel and walking the winter beach. After all everybody knows that when you hear the weather reports from over the state that the Outer Banks always has the highest temperature.

I had things really squared away at home as I always did before I left. My two oldest boys were in school and could get themselves back and forth and in general take care of themselves until my husband got home in the afternoon. My youngest boy was taken care of by a lady who came in and stayed all day when I was away from home for the week jobs. They were all healthy and happy when they waved us off to our exciting adventure.

On the way down, Mandy and I noticed that it was getting very cloudy and looking ominous in a heavy grey sort of way. Also it was so cold that it took our breaths when we got out of the car to have a hamburger for lunch. By the time we got to Manteo and then Nags Head it was clear by the churning water in the inlet by the causeway leading to the island that a storm was at least a possibility. We rode down the beach for a few miles before coming to the town of Kitty Hawk where we found our motel looking elegant, but cold and empty. As it turned out we were the only guests that whole week. We were outnumbered by the staff. They had so much room that we found ourselves being given two adjoining rooms which made up an efficiency apartment with cooking equipment, utensils, refrigerator, and the works. Both rooms had a heater, one permanent and one moveable. They were turned on only after we arrived and it looked like a long time was going to pass before teeth chattering would not be on our agenda. In the meantime we had decided to take a second story room so we could look out and see the ocean.

By the time we got our portable typewriters, clothes, books, and various other paraphernalia up the stairs we had warmed up considerably. We had noticed that right across the road was a restaurant that looked local and cheap and probably good. It was the only thing besides one filling station and one other restaurant we had seen open on the whole beach.

The principal and his wife had invited us for supper that first night and gave us explicit directions for getting to their house, which was a bit inland. We started out and thought we had taken all the right turns, but apparently we missed one, because in the dark and cold we seemed to just keep going long past the time when we should have arrived. The road was getting narrow and we only saw a few lights here and there. Suddenly, we came into a village of sorts, but there didn't seem to be anybody there and all the lights were off. Mandy and I finally admitted to each other that we were not on the right road, and if we weren't then where in the world were we, and were we getting ready to run into the ocean at the next turn. If we were on the road we thought we might be on, that's exactly what had to happen, as the island ended as far as the map was concerned at the last intersection we passed.

Just as we were really getting spooked, we saw a small house with one light on. Leaving Mandy in the car with the motor running in case of a fast get-away, I went to the door and knocked. I saw a familiar sight for the North Carolina coast. A man and his wife were baiting crab lines by tying cut-up salted eel into slip knots at intervals on a long rope. They stopped what they were doing long enough to give me to understand that we had made the wrong turn and they waved their hands in the general direction of where we should go back to.

In fact, there was not but one way to go back, along the same narrow road we had taken to get there. Heading back we realized that we were running about an hour late to supper and that my car had about three gallons of gas left in it if we were extremely lucky. If I had not had Mandy in the car I honestly believe I would have stopped by the side of the road and had a small nervous breakdown before continuing. There is no place in North Carolina more remote, more desolate, more deserted in the winter than right where we were that night, late, cold, and running out of gas. No lights, no people, and no signs to even indicate that we were indeed still in the world.

Mercifully for all concerned we soon came back to a spot we recognized, made all the right turns and finally came to the principal's house where the roast was overdone from its wait in the oven and the principal was on the verge of sending out the highway patrol. After all we would have been easy to find. We were the only two fools wandering around the end of the world, which we later found out was the fishing village of Duck. The whole population there made its living from striking out before dawn to fish and that's why they were all asleep and all the lights were doused by nine o'clock. We were told we were lucky we found anyone awake to steer us back and that about a mile and a half down the road we would have found ourselves on the sand which leads down the path to the end of the island into the ocean. Don't worry, we were told, you would have just gotten stuck in the sand and wouldn't really have run off the island into the water. Mandy just gave me a look which I translated as latent hysteria.

After a delightful meal, the principal led us down to a self-service gas station and took care of that problem. Making sure that we could find our way back to the motel without further episode we told him good night and started back.

Amazingly enough we saw a small store open on the way back and stopped to get some soup and stuff like that so that we could cook in our apartment if we felt tired one night or if the local fare wasn't up to what we wanted. We were looking forward to going to the school, with its enthusiastic principal and its particular make-up which was all the kids on the island from kindergarten through seventh grade. Getting back to the motel we realized that the two heaters were not going to get the two rooms warm enough to even sleep in, so we moved the portable one into my room where the permanent one was and Mandy moved into my room for the night. Outside the wind was literally howling and the extreme cold was creeping into all corners of the room despite the best efforts of storm doors and heaters and heavy drapes. The last thing Mandy muttered before we went to sleep was, I thought this place was supposed to be warm in the winter.

The next thing she said was when the alarm went off the next morning and she got up to open the drapes and peer out onto the beach. What she said was, "I know it's just the sand swirling, but I swear it looks like it's snowing on the beach." And it was snow and it was snowing and it did snow all that day. Five lovely inches of snow with the ocean in an absolute rage. Neither of us had ever seen anything like it before.

However, when the principal called us and said the school was, of course, closed, it began to dawn on me that we might be there for a while in those motel rooms with no students. How long do you think it will last and how long will the schools be closed and do you think we should go home, were some of my questions. Well, it was supposed to last all day, and probably the next day the schools would also be closed, and maybe by Wednesday we could find the students in residence again. As far as leaving and coming back was concerned, that was out of the question because the storm covered all of North Carolina, and besides, the causeway, the only way off the island, was closed because of ice.

Obviously the only thing to do was to sit back and drink soup or go across the way and eat and look out at the storm on the beach and relax. We were as stuck as one could be.

We were excited about the snow on the beach. The first thing we had to find out was is it possible to go out and walk on the beach in the falling snow. It wasn't. The wind was so severe that it cut into our eyes with a blinding effect. We could barely walk back and forth to the little cafe across the road which was, remarkably enough, open for business. It was all great fun and real adventure and we loved getting all bundled up and stomping around.

I had just gotten back and settled from an all-time great breakfast when the phone rang. It was my husband. His greeting words were something like, "What in the hell am I supposed to do with all these poets stuck all over the place?" In my thinking about our situation I had forgotten that for a number of reasons I had five other poets out that week. All were in coastal areas where it never snowed in January. They weren't quite as coastal as we were and the snow was reaching deep proportions. The ones who left on Sunday were in the same fix Mandy and I were in. The ones who were to leave Monday morning were still at home, thank goodness. The only thing I could tell the others who were calling was to get home as soon as possible and fix a return date with the schools before they left. Obviously they would not be teaching at all that week as the snow was reaching ten and fifteen inches in some places. Before some could get home it cost the program several hundred dollars to house and feed them and then pay travel back when they had rescheduled. I was exceedingly glad that I didn't have many out.

Then it occurred to me that my husband was home and not at work. As it turned out, no sooner had I left home than two of the boys started throwing up and running a fever. He suspected that the third one would come down with the plague at any moment. Also, there was no way that the woman who kept the baby could even leave her house. So my worst fears and Jim's about my trips away were realized. I had left home and he was in the position of having to stay home and nurse while I was stuck in a blizzard two hundred miles away. Fortunately the next day he was able to put snow chains on the car and go get the lady to take the kids so he could get back to work. But they were all sick all week and the snow in Raleigh was an unheard of and unbelievable fifteen inches.

For someone who is from one of the northern states, this seems, I am sure, a ridiculous situation to cause so much panic, but you have to realize that in the southern states, a snowfall like this doesn't happen often and it doesn't pay the cities to have the kinds of equipment necessary to clear the roads and highways off with the necessary dispatch. When it snows a few inches everything closes down until a day or two later, but when it snows fifteen inches nobody even knows where to begin.

Back in Kitty Hawk, Mandy and I were trying to figure out the best way to handle the classes when the school reopened. Mandy had originally planned merely to sit in on my classes and help a bit. Now it became a possibility that her role would be greatly expanded. When Tuesday came and the schools were indeed still closed, it became a certainty. We divided the classes between us with me taking five a day and Mandy taking four a day and that way we could reach slightly more students than we had planned to reach in the first place. Of course, it meant that some of the kids would have two poetry classes a day, but that couldn't be helped.

We approached the principal with the idea and he was in favor of anything we wanted to do and would help us rearrange the classes any way at all. Fortunately the school was small and could be turned over to poetry for three days and the other subjects could be picked up on later. In other words they were flexible enough to change things around. Mandy and I would work out her schedule and what would be taught or tried in her classes and mine each night before we went to the school the next day. It was like working out a gigantic crossword puzzle. We worked as hard as we could push ourselves that three days we had.

At the end of the week, even though I had made it clear to the principal that he only owed us for three days, he paid us for the full five days. I split it down the middle with Mandy. She deserved it. Needless to say, she learned a lot and the kids benefited at the same time. I was glad she had done the homework and reading I'd sent her before we started out.

Going home we realized the full impact of how bad the storm really had been. Everywhere snow was piled in great mounds beside the road. I was hoping they wouldn't find some of my poets under them when the spring thaw came!

My husband was ecstatic to see me, as were the children and the dog. What were the drops of blood doing in the hall I wondered. Could it be that the dog was in heat. Could it be that neither my husband nor anyone else had noticed that our gorgeous full-blooded golden retriever had been out frolicking in the snow in a promiscuous manner? It was true, she had, and evidently more than once, because in the spring thaw what was found were fourteen black and white puppies one morning being cared for by our red dog in the basement.

Mandy and I started the free classes in one of my children's schools the next week. Monday I started to feel a bit bad and by that afternoon I had my final souvenir from the previous week, the London flu, and was in bed ten days while Mandy finished up. I mean, why not, she was doing everything else. The final blow was when she left to go to the other city to work with the other poet. She only got halfway there before heading for her own home where she spent ten days with the London flu before going back to Salem College. I suppose that would be a good way to convince any college students champing at the bit to get out of school to stay where they were!

I'll admit that the previous story was not of an average week, but it had its moments of being average and smacks somewhat of many other experiences other poets had during the course of the program. As luck would have it, it snowed again about a month later, that time only on the coast, and caught two poets down east on Friday before they could leave town and they had to stay the weekend before being able to drive home. Fortunately, we had emergency funds in our budget to cover all the days our poets spent in motels trying to leave or teach or whatever. It reminded me of the story one of my friends told about when he was working in the program in South Carolina and got caught in a motel room for two days with only a Gideon Bible and a picture of "Custer's Last Stand."

Amazingly enough, we only lost one school from the snow situation. They and the poet were never able to get back together on a date. Of course all of this threw my best laid plans upside down and took several weeks to straighten out. It was not the only reason that I was having problems with schedules. Some of the poets had other jobs that got a bit tight and one moved to another state and two dropped out for personal reasons and I got two or three new poets in the program. The changes got almost as rapid and hard to follow during February and March as they had been early in the fall. But then just as suddenly things calmed down again and everybody was buzzing along.

I went to some other schools in the course of the year. I went to one which I thought would be great. As it turned out it was a cold week both for me and for them. Somehow everything went wrong from the beginning and it turned into the worst week I ever had anywhere before or since. I even got awful evaluations on my work from the one teacher involved. I saw the principal once to speak to and some of the other teachers in the lounge. When I had the workshop the teachers sat around with their arms crossed and seemed to have only negative things to ask and say. The kids were waiting with an "I'll dare you to tell us anything" attitude from day one. By day two I was going home every night cross as hell, hoping to resolve the whole mess as quickly as possible.

I learned a lot of valuable lessons from that school, however painful. I learned to look very carefully at any bad evaluations that came in on poets from other schools. Had they run into something unsolvable like I had or were they really doing a lousy job. I also got a big lesson in humility. I found that I couldn't go in and "pull it off" no matter what, that on occasion no matter how well you've done in other places, or no matter how well prepared you are, there are going to be certain situations which you can't make good.

On the other hand, just a few weeks from then I went to a junior high school in the town where I was born and reared (except we were "raised," by the whole town) and had a delightful experience. I saw faces that were familiar enough to give me a spooky feeling. Was I really seeing the faces of my former classmates? No, just the delightful blending of a child where two of them had married. Now I was teaching that blend.

I also had some dealings with my former teachers and found that despite what I might have thought at the time they really did always expect me to turn out all right. I heard all about how I was as a student and it was so much in contrast with what I had been thinking all these years. It is amazing how we can make up our lives as we go along until some day something like this happens. I found that I really was always a reader and writer and good student, when I had always pictured myself as falling into this role when I was thirty and started serious writing for the first time. Oh no, they assured me, you always sat and wrote stuff in the back of the room. One teacher reminded me of how I edited *Julius Caesar* in the sixth grade and got a group together and directed them in a small performance for the class. So I had once had the gall to edit Shakespeare.

Back in the office, we had some schools around the state who wanted to get a poet and finance the week by themselves. We helped six schools with this by getting them someone and sending the guidelines and all to keep them within the framework of the program. Any school who did this was eligible to send in student work for the anthology. This was a good sign to us that some of the communities, with a bit of help, might eventually pick up the program on their own.

Very soon the program seemed to be coming to an end. Despite a few bizarre occurrences the program had been successful. Most of the poets and schools had fulfilled the evaluation and booklet obligations and we sent out the following memo to those few who had not.

MEMORANDUM

TO: Schools Participating in the Poetry-in-the-Schools Program

FROM Ardis Kimzey, Coordinator
       Poetry-in-the-Schools Program
       Division of Cultural Arts

    I have found the checked item(s) to be missing from your file. We are most anxious to begin writing our evaluation and to begin this year's anthology. Please have the missing item(s) in to us within the next week or call to let us know when we may expect them.

    Thank you for your cooperation.

( ) Student and teacher evaluations

( ) Poetry booklets

Due to the strict way the guidelines had been followed it didn't take long to get these errant items into the office.

During the month of May, I was able to put the anthology together to go to the printers and to get the evaluations together. Because of the material coming in throughout the year and filing system and so forth that we had, the evaluative process, although time consuming, was relatively easy to get moving and together. Also the anthology was about twice as easy as the year before when none of us knew anything.

Pat Bowers did the cover again, Notie Brents the typing and Jim Jackman the dickering with the printer. One thing was different however. During the year I had had the anthologies coming in on a staggered basis for a purpose. It gave me an opportunity to read all the poems in all the anthologies from the sixty-seven schools involved without so many at once that I would drive my car off a building. As I read each book, I would check the good poems and put a paperclip on the top of the page where I had checked a poem. Then when I got through I'd go back and make sure I didn't have more than ten chosen. If I did, I'd narrow it down to ten. Then I got a Board of Editors and they spent two days going through the books just looking at the poems I had marked and that the poet in that school had marked. Most of the poets had taken the time to mark their favorite poems from a school in an identical booklet which they sent to me. I made a notation of these markings in the master booklet I was working with. The editors (there were four) had a different color pen to mark with. They marked the ones they liked best from the paper-clipped pages. I didn't give them a particular number to mark or not mark, just trusting to fate that it would all come out approximately right.

After this was done I went back through the books and put a red circle around the poems that had two editor's marks in addition to either the poet's mark or mine. That way at least three people passed on each poem. Then Notie took the books as I finished with them and started typing the individual poems. We both checked the finished poem for errors in every way possible and when we were convinced that they were all right, I took the scissors and cut them out.

Believe it or not, what I was doing was to give the book visual balance. I piled all the poems of the same size together. Then I put all the numbered pages (we had a set number) out on four long tables put end to end. Next, I Scotch-taped the poems on the pages in the square laid out for them. They almost came out even, using three short fat poems on one page and one big poem on another and one long skinny poem and three tiny ones on another page and so on. It was nerve-wracking because I had no earthly idea how it would turn out until it did. Nevertheless it turned out great and when the galleys came back they were much better than the year before, which was to make some compromises. Printers just don't like poetry manuscripts and it's best to plan ahead to do major battle with the best of them to get the poems to look right.

When the anthology, *I Don't Need You, Rod McKuen, Good-Bye,* came out it was a smash. The newspapers gave it good reviews all over the state. We once again sent it to the schools and the kids who had poems in it, but we also sent it to some major publishers to see if any of them would be interested in re-publishing it. They weren't, and to my knowledge, they still haven't published more than a handful of books along these lines. It looks as if they would investigate this possibility, at least in the school divisions, since students like other students' work and can relate to it.

The first year it never occurred to me that we would have "lifted" material in the anthology. But sure enough it was called to my attention that a haiku from the *World Book* had found its tiny way into the anthology. Fortunately, the material was old enough to be in the public domain. It caused a great to-do among some folks who weren't even involved in the program and I wound up with the feeling that they wanted the child lashed in public. On the other hand I felt that probably an honest error had been made. Many poets—I've done it myself—make the statement, "Go home and bring me back a poem tomorrow if the spirit moves you." Sometimes the kids might think they can bring back anything they want to. And everyone who works with kids knows they have no compunctions about copying a poem they like in their notebooks and not putting the author's name by it. They don't plan to pass it off as theirs, they just don't really think to put the poet's name by it. They like it, copy it, and that's that. I have an idea that this is what happened that year. Then too, sometimes the poet gets a sheaf of papers and something could easily be picked up by mistake.

This year, I had a board of editors that was forewarned of the problem from the year before. Nonetheless a poem by Edgar Guest got right by us smooth as silk. Still I never did anything about it because I'd rather the kid have the benefit of the doubt. I felt a bit better when it was discovered that one of the winning poems in a great magazine for kids named *Cricket* was a bit familiar and they had to make all manner of retractions. Ultimately, I suppose there's no way to guard against such a thing one hundred percent.

The evaluations from the teachers and poets from the year pointed up the strengths and weaknesses of the program very well. From them and from my own observations as a teacher in the program and from the view from my desk I thought I could make some reasonable recommendations for the next year. Both Jim Hall, head of the Division of Cultural Arts, and I knew that some changes would have to be made. For one thing I had been paid a good enough price for my work during the year as an inexperienced person, but now I was worth a bit more to someone, if not Jim Hall. He didn't want to spend more money for administration and I felt that I couldn't do the same job for the same price again. We both recognized that the hours of work the program needed far outreached the amount of money he was willing to pay an outside administrator.

Also, we both realized that the cost in the office of running the program with that many poets and schools to keep up with was affecting the inner-office funds for budget items like telephone calls, Xeroxing and secretarial help. The permanent sections of the department were having to cut back on these items in order for the poetry program, which was only a component of another program, to have funds. In this division there were the full time art, drama, visual arts, and music consultants who ran those programs for the entire State. But before the recommendations for change, we took a long look at the evaluations that came in from out in the field.

The teachers in the schools seemed to be able to give more valuable evaluations than the students or the administrators, which is to be expected. The only thing I had hoped to get from the administrators was whether or not there was a significant problem area. The teachers were working with the poets and could be more involved with them from day to day. For the most part, the poets who worked well in one place worked well in all places. On occasion a poet would run into a problem school and between the poet and teacher evaluation I could usually tell where the breakdown occurred.

Some of the poets were average workers as will always be the case in a program using so many poets. If a school were happy with that then all was well. If they expected gangbusters and a super performer then they'd express their disappointment by saying something like "the poet seemed unprepared" or "wasn't good with the students." However, I found most of the teacher evaluations to be pretty accurate. As it turned out, we had four or five real losers, about four mediocre poet teachers, and the rest were solid good. Out of thirty-four poets, that's not a bad average. From the time the committee met back in the fall, I felt I could have picked out most of the troublemakers but there were two or three of them who surprised even me. Perhaps the solution was the one I suggested when I left, use fewer poets, be sure of your ground with those you use.

The teachers consistently cited the need for more time, both during the poet's day and during the program in general. They also felt a need for a follow-up week sometime during the year. Most of them hated the paperwork surrounding the whole enterprise. The anthology work and the student evaluations seemed to be the thorniest points. I felt sure that we could eliminate most of the student evaluations the next year. As long as National Endowment felt the way it did about samples of the student work, and I felt the way I did about the student work at least being mimeographed, then it didn't seem possible to do anything about the amount of work involved in collecting and reproducing the students' poems.

I could sympathize with the poet walking into a strange school and trying to work with 120 students and read and mark all their poems. Obviously they were at a saturation point. On the other hand, I could also sympathize with the teacher coordinators in the schools. They were, as a rule, extremely competent, forward-thinking teachers, which meant they were already probably taking on more than was humanly possible to accomplish when the poetry project came dancing out of the wings.

It remains a dilemma. On the other hand, I have seen in the past few years some of the parents in the schools come forward and take the anthology over for the school. This is a "best of all possible worlds" solution if it can be done. It affords everyone some breathing room and includes the parents in the project too.

The school secretary is not the one to push this project on. She is busy running the school. All the excuses, throwing ups, goings and comings, checking in the supplies, and so on, go over and through her desk. In her spare time, she is trying to protect the principal like many nurse-receptionists trying to protect and conceal a good many doctors. Anyone who overlooks the fact that the school secretary is someone important to his or her success in the schools is an idiot. Whether it's the principal you want to find or the masking tape, she is your key.

The poets came up with many good workable changes for the program for the next year. Most of them were details which could easily be incorporated into the plans. Some were overall changes. There were a few suggestions, or maybe I should say, observations, that will have to remain as the status quo as long as the schools are set up the way they are.

In looking back over the evaluations for the purpose of this book, I am again amazed at the consistency with which the program had success, and with the enthusiasm of the poets and the teachers involved, and also at the great dedication shown to the particulars of the program by the poets and teachers alike. Time after time, the evaluations by the poets stated that the coordinating teachers had gone above and beyond normal expectations in preparing for their visits. For the most part the whole week was a good experience for everyone involved. The things that went wrong seemed to be in certain schools where everything went wrong or with certain poets who simply weren't up to snuff. However, the poets did have suggestions and observations which should be noted here in case they may help some other system working on a similar program.

Finances cropped up again and again and the general consensus in the office was that it would be better to give the poets a set amount of money to pay for lodging and food and for the State Department to pay the mileage as reported. The expense sheets were a bother even though they had been simplified. My feeling at the beginning of the program was that some poets would wind up making more money than others if we did it that way. Certainly poets who worked at home would benefit. Also, I felt that maybe we could save a bit by piecing out the money. However, I changed my mind. There was a constant hassle with checking and rechecking the money and the expense sheets. It became more trouble than it was worth.

Then, there were the poets who thought the money paid them was ridiculously low and they were worth much more. In a couple of cases, I agreed and in a couple I thought they were being paid too much, so that came out even. But there was some talk about the money and there still is and there always will be. The trick to that is to insist that the poet not work in the program in the first place if the money is not satisfactory. For instance, I now personally have a price for weeks in town and one for work out of town. I state it in a friendly way and don't budge. I go or don't go, but we're all happy or at least satisfied in one way or another about the money.

This brings up something about the hiring of the poets I feel compelled to throw in at this point. If a poet has a disposition that tends toward evil temper or prima donna inclinations, rest assured that a week in this program is not going to solve the problem. It's like getting older; all our faults intensify. So, if you start out with such a poet expect it to go all downhill from Monday to Friday. This is not a program that pampers anyone. Everybody works like hell and sometimes the poet will go in and find that no preparations have been made and no arrangements that make any sense and they have to get up and take charge and do the best they can to pull it out of the fire. This is no place for a bad disposition or famous poets with further illusions of grandeur. There is no guarantee that the best laid plans will do a particle of good given some circumstances in some schools.

Two of the suggestions for change that were repeatedly mentioned were certainly my fault. One was that the elementary school students couldn't understand the evaluations they were supposed to fill out. Well, of course they couldn't and as soon as I got that suggestion in on the first evaluation, I sent out memos to all the elementary schools to stop the evaluation process for the students. That was a good example of unclear thinking on my part, and I was glad to have it called to my attention from the beginning. Some of the schools did continue it however just for interest's sake to see what the younger ones would say. The other suggestion was that the teachers and poets needed more in the way of orientation at the conference and that the long afternoon spent with the poets reading from their work could be better spent in small groups talking about the program and what to expect in the school and what was necessary to both parties for happiness.

The poets found most of the teachers overworked, involved to the point of not even having a toilet break during the day, and having to oversee students during lunch. It was a revelation for those who hadn't been in the public schools before. They could also sympathize with the teachers who complained that they never got any school work done for all the other activities. Despite good planning, these classes would be interrupted by students coming and going from band and P.E. and afternoon basketball games. The poets also found in some schools that their students were having difficulty getting their permission slips signed to come to poetry class by teachers all steamed up to be difficult. A lot of students were consistently late for the same reason. This could have been through a lack of communication with the teachers of other subjects and the teachers in the English department. Or it could have been due to simple orneriness.

The schedule hassle I had with the schools before the poets arrived seemed to have its just rewards. Almost every poet had a suitable schedule. Even so, they had some suggestions. Some wanted Friday off to deal with the volume of poems received during the week and to get them ready for the anthology. Some would have liked to return to the schools to do follow-up work. Some suggested something that they knew would be almost impossible from a distance, which was that the program might work better if it could be done one day a week for five weeks instead of such a concentrated week.

The best schedule seemed to be two classes in the morning with a short break, then another morning class, lunch, and the last class. A few warnings were issued. One was not to take over already existing classes because you're treated too much like a substitute. Another was to make sure that the kids volunteer for the classes and know for sure what they're getting into.

One of the poets suggested something that I like but have never seen done, and that is to have a summer workshop for those students whom the poets in the different schools recommend for further study. Another suggested that the poets in the schools should concentrate more on quality rather than quantity. If a student has a good poem going, why not let him work on it all week. Several reported a practice in some of the schools of having the kids who were in the workshops go back to their rooms and tell the other kids about what happened and get them writing poems too.

There were many things about the program that the poets uniformly reported they liked. I won't go into the obvious ones but two of them offer valuable insights. One was that every poet who had a room of his own (shades of Virginia Woolf) thought it extremely helpful to his week's success. Another was that the anthology we had put out the year before, *Tenderness,* was invaluable as a collection to use in teaching and to read from. Hearing work from other kids generated an enthusiasm that the best work from adults had not. Especially among the younger kids it was an excitement for them to hear work by other third and fourth graders.

In the few schools where the poets felt they were working in a vacuum, there was great despair at leaving their kids after the week was over. One of the poets reported in her evaluation that one of her students had said, "I guess this is the last poem I'll ever write. There won't be anyone to show it to when you're gone." Hopefully those incidences were few.

One of our fine poets working in the program, Richard Vela, had an excellent statement to make in his evaluation that I'll pass on here.

Comments on the program—
Positive: The idea of the whole thing is tremendous. Although I must admit that when it started last year, I wasn't so sure about it. I wondered about some of the kinds of things Rod Cockshutt brought

up in his column in the Raleigh paper: who says who is or isn't a poet (and all the literary-political problems that issue suggests), and further who is or isn't the kind of poet one wants to put into a classroom with a group of elementary students. O.K. so now after the program has been going on for a year or two and I have worked in it myself and talked with several others who have, the answer I find leads me to a new problem. The answer is that it doesn't seem to make that much difference as far as the students go. Who comes in isn't quite as important as the fact that for one week someone did come in who said he (or she) was a poet and who seemed to care enough about it to take it seriously and who was willing to work with them and talk to them. So my problem is this:

Negative: The fact that it *can* be most anyone, however solid or valid or not his claims to being a good writer. Koch in *Wishes, Lies and Dreams* casually mentions several times that he has suggested various exercises to classroom teachers and then goes on to discuss their success or lack of it with a particular exercise. The point then is that if the classroom teacher, who is not a writer, can make it on the strength of the exercises, what exactly do *we* do that makes us worth more? Could you send somebody who knew only what you told him about writing and who came prepared with a set of lesson plans or techniques, could you send somebody like this into a classroom, tell the students he was a poet and get away with it? The point I'm making has nothing to do with the quality of the people that are being sent into the classrooms, but with the self-assessment that a poet needs to make before he enters the class: what is there that I'm going to do that is going to make a real difference, that could be done only by me because of my commitment to poetry and what is the media for whatever it is: is my real means of communication the exercises, the individual comments I make to a student, a combination of things? The point is then finally that we need to give some thought to the difference between gimmick poetics and honest poetics. All of this is not really a criticism but a consideration that I felt myself making all the time that I was with the classes: the awareness not so much of a problem but of an issue.

I would be willing to stake myself out that this issue will continue to be debated as long as there is a Poetry-in-the-Schools Program. Much will be said on both sides and there is the good possibility that nothing will ever be settled. I personally go with the idea that there is a bit of all things he mentioned. I think you have to have some material to work with, whether it be exercise material or poems, or personal observations, or combinations thereof. I think you have to be willing to go in and honestly share the person you are with the students. And I think your commitment to whatever you believe about poetry has to be so strong that it shows in what you do as a kind of integrity. The combination of all that makes your week a separate entity that never happens the same way twice, because you never have the same students, sometimes not even from one day to the next. And sometimes I'm a different person from one day to the next. All of this could easily add up in absolute and total chaos unless you have an underlying personal faith in yourself and in every other separate human being. Then whatever happens is okay.

We are now at the end of the year when I ran the program for the State Department of Public Instruction. I learned a lot. Everybody did. It was time for me to make a move one way or another. I made my recommendations for the next year and stated my price for carrying them out. By that time I had made it clear to Jim Hall that my price was solid and that I was so convinced of certain things that my recommendations were not up to much change either. He didn't want to pay that much to an administrator, which I have gone into earlier and some of the ideas I had still didn't give him the coverage he wanted. I was going to believe to the end of my days that more concentration was needed and he still believed in spreading the joy. So we parted ways, but in understanding and friendship. We have continued to work together from time to time. He calls me to brainstorm which I enjoy and maybe in the next year or two we may put our heads together on some projects we're both interested in.

In the meantime here are the suggestions I made for the following year before I left:

1. That the week long residencies continue but with some eye to a follow-up of maybe even a week if the money could be found.

2. That we used the same guidelines, discontinuing the student evaluations.

3. That we try to finance teacher workshops in mass at two college campuses on opposite ends of the state for a few days, pulling in our best teacher poets to teach teachers more effective ways of dealing with kids in the creative writing process.

4. That the poets be given a set amount of money to cover stipends and lodging and food and that we pay mileage separately from our office.

5. That the poets be chosen by the department by those people who had had contact with them and knew whom to be

dependable as best we could ascertain from the preceding year.

6. That fewer poets be used to cut down on the paper-work, but that enough poets be used to keep the program exciting.

7. That the State Department still keep a close watch over the program to ascertain that the schools and the poets were living up to their responsibilities.

8. That the state-wide anthology be discontinued and a really nice looking magazine be started that would come out three times a year for the students to submit to from all over the state. I felt that if the quality were high, libraries would subscribe to it and we would have a ready market for sales. That money plus some from the grant would keep it going.

9. That we find some way to identify and use more minority poets in the program.

10. That we investigate the possibility of starting an apprentice program in order to have a continuation of quality teaching.

11. That the conference at the beginning of the year have more orientation and small group activities.

12. That the large school systems be given more incentive to start their own programs.

Some of these ideas were acted upon. Some were ignored. Some were changed or watered down. Some new ideas were formulated after I left. Any program of this magnitude is going to have its ins and outs and its good points and bad. There is no way to do all that needs to be done and all of us can only do what we think is best. I decided when I left not to try to evaluate the administration of the program from afar without knowing what was really happening and I'll stick to that decision. I do know that a grant program has been started whereby large school systems apply for money to run their own programs. I myself acted on a request from a local arts orga-nization, the Raleigh Cultural Center, to get a grant for them and to run a local program of Writers-in-Residence, which is what I did the next year.

II

TEACHING METHODS
AND
ATTITUDES

Chapter 4

ELMER'S GLUE, SCOTCH TAPE, POETRY, AND OTHER WAYS OF PUTTING THE WORLD TOGETHER

"The student should come to know the teacher, which is a thousand times better than knowing what the teacher knows."
—Wendell Berry

One summer my oldest son was away at camp. Eager to hear all about his activities, I wrote my first letter laced with questions. In his return letter he said, "By the way, in response to your questions: yes, no, sometimes, maybe and never." Needless to say, I was soundly thwarted in my efforts to gain information.

Now, I don't want to do the same thing here. But there are always questions people ask me about working with kids and poetry that seem to me to demand this same kind of scattered response. And the parts of the response can be interchanged at different times and in different situations.

Of course the major question always asked is can you teach a student how to write poetry. I think probably the answer is no. The answer would be "no" because I can go into any junior high school and if I have all the students who in their whole lives might write poetry and those students have never been taught by a poet before, I can tell (and would even lay bets on it) which ones have the talent and which ones will probably make it if they care hard enough. Now that's a lot of "if's," but there they are.

I do think that most kids will show their affinity for and talent for writing by then if they're going to. Now there may be kids who care more about football or math who would make astounding writers, but they will never be interested in writing so you can't really count on them. Having the proper talent doesn't automatically mean that you're going to be driven to the wall with it racing through your head and coursing through your veins until you cry "Uncle" and write. That's a nice romanticized version of the writer; and one I might add that I try to rid my students of as soon as possible. None of that matters unless you give your talent the proper attention.

So, (1) THE TEACHER CAN TEACH THE STUDENT TO GIVE THE PROPER ATTENTION TO HIS ABILITY. There are many students who don't know they have ability until you tell them and that is all a part of Number One. Also there are students who think they have ability because they can write poems like the ones they see covering the poetry sections in most bookstores and whose author shall go nameless here because we all know who it is. Those students you have to spend a bit more time with because first of all you have to show them what an image is and then you have to see if they can put it into practice. But it is nonetheless a part of paying attention. Sometimes you can pick out students like this in the fifth or sixth grade. They are the ones who already have poetry books they have written ready for you when you arrive. Mostly the poems are metered and rhymed, but usually the student can be reformed in a few sessions.

The next thing a teacher can do is (2) PROVIDE GOOD POEMS AND MANY OF THEM AND IN MANY DIFFERENT STYLES FOR THE STUDENT TO READ AND PONDER OVER. Now right away everybody's going to jump me and say how can you tell what's a good poem and how are you going to ascertain which poets to put in front of your students. And I'll say, yes, no, sometimes, etc. because I subscribe to about twenty little magazines from all over the country plus most of the ones in our state, and to *American Poetry Review,* which is supposed to have a variety of people represented in it, and I have a whole library of poetry books gathered from brochures I get and from my favorite bookstores in Washington, D.C., San Francisco, and New York. And not only do I get all these; I also actually read them, and for those reasons and more I think I can provide my students with a good experience in a variety of poetry. I have bought on numerous occasions books which I curled my lip over, but which I had heard were considered good in some quarters. I bought them for students to look at and read if the poetry appealed to them.

I will have to admit that I'm not that fair in most of the classes about what I read, because I'm trying in most cases to read poems which show something about poetry that I'm trying to get across that particular day. It is only natural to use poems in that instance which I admire and know well. I will also readily admit that at this point, I'm running about two years behind on knowing the new young (or old) poets. Teaching takes your time away from learning and I don't have my nose in the "littles" quite as much as I used to. However, I'm not too far behind and it doesn't seem to bother most of my students who are still reading Whitman and Cummings at best.

Some of what I've said is certainly for the older student. But there is one more thing you can do which applies to all students and that is open their doors or (3) OPEN STUDENT IMAGINATION AND LET THEM KNOW THAT ANYTHING IS POSSIBLE, NOT ONLY IN THEIR WORK BUT IN THEIR LIVES. I've seen students in very tight classroom situations become alive with knowing that here is an adult who is saying what they've had the audacity to dream and giggle about. And some of them never forget that experience no matter how hard that classroom closes down again after you leave. And I've seen the opposite end of that stick where the classroom is open and the kids and teacher are alive and kicking and to show them the refinement of the creative process and where it can take them is yet another joy.

There is a fourth unofficial item which goes something like this. All of the above could be done by a really on-the-ball teacher in the classroom, so why do we need to spend such high sums on a writer-in-residence. Well, first of all most teachers are not competent in that way, and they are the first to admit this. They went to school in a time, which could be a few years ago, or now, when contemporary poetry was not taught. And second of all, most of them are educators and not poets. The final thrust of the Poets-in-Schools Program as I see it is that you can give the students all the above, but from the viewpoint and sensibility of a practicing poet. The poet, by virtue of his profession, is going to bring things into the classroom that a teacher, no matter how fine, is not going to be able to give to the students.

I do believe however that teachers can be taught to work with kids in poetry in certain ways and that they can be made aware of the changes going on in the field of poetry and that all of this will help the students. I have given teacher workshops for the State Department of Public Instruction, separate from my weeks in the schools, where teachers came just to see if they could get material and ideas about working with kids in poetry, to update their knowledge and concepts. I know that these teachers went home with lots of ideas and names of books and names of contemporary poetry anthologies and if they used them would have much better classes in language arts. In this situation, if the poet never comes the kids are still better off and if a poet does come, the week moves along in giant steps.

Probably at the heart of training teachers to work with kids in poetry is to increase their awareness of contemporary poetry. Most smart teachers, when they see what the changes are, can put them into play in their classrooms. If a teacher can understand contemporary poetry and understand the concepts behind it then he or she can readily understand the exercises that bring these concepts into play. This is totally necessary in teacher sessions because if you just throw out a number of cute and interesting exercises and that's all, then the teachers go back using gimmicks with the class with no underlying understanding of what is really going on.

Despite the fourth idea, the first three remain basically my answer to what I can do for my students. If in the process, it "teaches" them to write poetry then so be it. But those three things I'll stand by—attention to ability, example, and expansion of awareness.

The last two can apply to any student whether that student has writing ability or not. By example they can learn enough about poetry to appreciate it the rest of their lives and by becoming more open they can learn much about themselves and other people. So, I don't apologize for teaching any class of students whether they are poets on the hoof or just a student, any student, sitting in my class for a week.

A lot of people teaching right now are all hung up about whether or not to use exercise material, that is, stuff like Kenneth Koch or Ron Padgett or some of the other great-white-fathers-in-the-sky of poetry teaching. As for me I have no qualms whatsoever about using such material if it gets me and the kids where I think we should be. Some purists worry at night, no doubt interrupting their sleep, about whether color and sound exercises will cause their changes to become gimmick machines. I will have to admit to resting easy.

What I do worry about is liking an idea so much that I will integrate it into my work with the kids without thinking it through as to

90

what it will ultimately accomplish. I suppose I've used everything I've read about or made up myself at least once just to see what would happen. Sometimes I will come across something that seems to have a lot to offer and I'll try it a number of times before it works in the way I had anticipated. Maybe I was using it at the wrong time or in the wrong place or with the wrong students. Sometimes I can tell right away that something is no good for my way of working, and I don't even bother with it again.

Finally, through the years, I have formulated in my own mind an idea about the use of exercise material which goes like this. An exercise is good if it leads to the discovery of an aspect of writing poetry which can later be assimilated into one's writing independent of the exercise itself or even the thought of it. For instance, if a student writes a color poem and later is writing another poem and color crops up as the right way to go about a line and she uses it naturally and without thinking about the color poem she wrote in my class, then it was a successful exercise (providing that color is what the poem needs!). If, however, a young poet writes nothing but color poems forever then the exercise is rotten. I have faith that the good young poet will forget the exercise and use the concept behind it and that the other students will write color poems until they tire of them and that will be that. Needless to say, behind this faith is the faith I must have in the exercises I use.

The system we use in North Carolina doesn't fit my idea of how the work ought to proceed. It is insane to go into a school for a week and then take off in a cloud of dust like the lone ranger, bringing ease for a while, then hi-hoing away never to return. From my own experience and from the evaluations I have seen, it is a most frustrating experience for everyone involved. However, it's the only system we had and it's the only one we have now until the changes being considered go into effect.

So, considering that we're working with a week's visit, no matter that it's under duress, let's see what can happen in that week. Since I've worked in all levels from kindergarten through high school, it's probably better for me to think in terms of age groups, although I have in mind the same ideas I want to get across. I want to teach the following concepts: (1) That poetry is accessible and not something that only a few can write, understand, and/or enjoy. (2) That poetry has to be crafted with certain tools and that the understanding of things, like color, the five senses, good words, imagination, special relationships, and comparative relationships brings a certain ease of movement in writing the poem.

I go about this in different ways with different age groups. It's like building a building except you have to realize that, practically speaking, only the foundation will ever be laid. You may work with some of these kids for a week and nobody will ever work with them in poetry again. This used to panic me into trying to cram too much into a week. Now I take my time and try to do a few things well and put lasting ideas into my students' heads.

Usually, I only have an hour or two at most with the kindergarten and first graders. When you're in a school and you can't see but so many students, the little ones are the first to be marked off the schedule. I normally wind up just dropping by to work with them a short while. Even so, I try to incorporate the same concepts in a condensed way.

Now, after all is said and done, one still has to get up in front of a class, usually one we have never laid eyes on until they come streaming through the door. The teacher introduces me as the poet and then, despite all the concepts and high-flown language, it becomes necessary to say something. And not only to say something, but something interesting enough to hold the attention of thirty wiggly very much alive first graders. At this point, I want something to use, some way of proceeding. Despite all the dissenters, I want a gilt-edged, well-used, "tried and found not wanting" exercise. The following is what I use now. The next time I go into a classroom it may be different. I'm always looking for a better way to teach.

The first thing I do is start a silly story. I say let's write a silly poem together. Somebody give me a first line. Well, it's usually about spring or baby ducks or something they think is appropriate for them to be doing. Immediately I'll suggest something like a story about a day in the life of a first grader. Then, I'll start by saying, "This morning I fell out of my bed which is the neck of an ostrich, onto my rug which is made up of a thousand earthworms." Well, you need go no further. They're off and running with the idea. Their story can take all sorts of turns and you're really only the referee and shaper by then. The teacher can usually be talked into taking dictation so you can work directly with what's happening.

(Silly stories)

FALSE POEM

Once upon a time there was a werewolf.
Who liked chocolate covered blood.
He saw a ship and he jumped on it.
And a dinosaur jumped on with him.
The ship thought it was in a tidal wave.
But really it was in a whale.
The people on the ship got some matches and burned
    a hole in the whale's tail and got out.
The ship went to land.
They got off the ship and they go visit a desert.
They saw a gorilla.
The gorilla squeezed the werewolf 'til he was dead.
All the people were happy because the werewolf
    wasn't any more.

Collaborative
J.W. York Elementary School
Raleigh, North Carolina

THE ANIMAL HOTEL

Animals live in a hotel.
It's a Holiday Inn.
The snakes sleep in the dresser drawers,
And they snore so loud, that the drawers
    fly open and shut all night long.
Elephants play ping-pong in the bathtub.
The balls go down the drain and come back up.
The birds make nests in the trash cans
    and sleep there.
The turtles sleep in the beds under
    the mattress,
And the tigers sleep on the roof.
They roar and make the hotel shake.
The monkey sleeps in the chimney,
So he can hang while he sleeps.
The pig sleeps behind the curtains,
And the bat sleeps on the windowsill.

The snails sleep in the pencil holders.
The mice sleep in the clock.
The penguin sleeps in the restaurant!
He eats all the cheese sandwiches.
In the daytime all the animals go to Darrel's.

Collaborative
J.W. York Elementary School
Raleigh, North Carolina

I move extremely fast in an hour with them, almost in double time or like a Charlie Chaplin movie. I also move about a lot physically, so that their eyes have to follow me just like their minds. After the imaginations are set off, I move right away to animals and sounds. What sound does a giraffe make? Nobody is too sure of course so they make up an appropriate sound. Soon the whole class is into the reproducing of this sound with great gusto. Okay, I'll shout over the roar. What does it sound like. Well, it sounds like a giraffe. But what else does it sound like? Oh, that is a different story, and they have to think about it for half a second before coming up with their responses. The teacher takes these down and we'll do about ten or twelve. (This also pleases teachers because of the nice lesson in phonics thrown in.)

ANIMAL SOUNDS

A cow goes Moo.
It sounds like the wind.
Blowing through the trees.
The duck says Quack, Quack.
It sounds like somebody crying.
The horse goes Nehihi.
It sounds like somebody laughing.
A sheep goes Baa, Baa.
It sounds like a machine gun.
A cat goes Meow, Meow.
It sounds like a zooming airplane.
A dog growling goes Rruff.
It sounds like a monster.
A snake goes Ssss-Ssss.
It sounds like a soft wind blowing.
An octopus goes Blup, Blup.

94

It sounds like water dripping.
A seal goes Arf, Arf.
It sounds like a dog.
A rooster goes Cock-a-doodle-do.
It sounds like an elephant.

Collaborative
J.W. York Elementary School
Raleigh, North Carolina

Next I might say, what does a buttercup dream of, a desert, a cow... and they get the message right away.

SLEEPING DREAMS

A giant dreams of little bitty girls
    with ribbons in their hair.
A whale dreams of Germans.
Jesus dreams of everybody.
Children dream of toys.
Caterpillars dream of soon being a butterfly.
Seeds dream of being a flower.
Flowers dream of soon opening up.
Whales dream of eating people.
Dogs dream of cats, cats dream of mice,
    mice dream of cheese.

Collaborative
J.W. York Elementary School
Raleigh, North Carolina

Then we think up all sorts of yummy colors like sunset red, jonquil yellow, night black and I put a list of the five senses on the board. What does sunset red smell like, taste like, and so on.

I used to end with the silly story that I now start with until I read Anne Martin's article in *Teachers & Writers Magazine,* Spring issue, 1973, about working with the first grade. Now I end by doing something she uses which is get the kids to write a poem about something they choose (still out loud and a collaborative) and tell about it as if the person they were writing for has never seen the thing. By this time of course, I have on the board sounds and dreams and colors and the five senses and I remind them to use all these when possible as they throw out their lines. Some remarkable work has come out of this.

SNOW

Snow is like fluffy little cotton balls
    falling down from the sky.
Snow tastes like an ice cube.
It makes your hands feel icy.
It can be wet like rain.
It's as light as flour.
It's as slippery as soap.
It smells like nothing.
You can pick it up and make it into a
    ball and throw it.
You can roll it into big balls, put them
    on top of each other and make a snowman.
You can get on your back in the snow and
    wave your arms up and down.
When you get up it looks like an angel.
Snow looks like clouds on the ground.

Collaborative
Aldert Root Elementary School
Raleigh, North Carolina

I have never worked with a first grade for a whole week and don't know whether this would be productive or not. I would think, off hand, that it would be better to work with them for a whole year to tell what would happen. I have worked with second, third and fourth grades for a week, however. In a week, I'll cover a number of things with them, but basically the same things I'll touch on briefly with the first grade in one hour.

We'll work on getting to know each other the first day, talking, letting them ask me questions, letting me ask them questions, finally letting them work on a poem or story together, usually oral. They think so much faster than they can write and I want them to think at the beginning without worrying about the big pencils and lined paper and spelling and all the things they get hung up with. So the first day they might not physically write at all.

The second day, I might bring paint samples that I got at the paint store (I know the local stores must think we're in a constant state of painting at our house). They like looking at the colors and there's much ado over which color they want, at which time some teachers freak out over the confusion. When the dust settles, I try to get them to work with the colors and the five senses together like the first grade except I put it all on the board and they write the things themselves, very slowly. I move among them as usual encouraging and commenting on what they're doing. I've found that they can use the colors this way better first than if they were to use either the colors or the five senses separately.

Gray
      is like
Tasting burned liver
Seeing a foggy bay
Hearing the whispering wind
Feeling depressed
Smelling the rain on our street after a hot sunny spell.

Amanda Kilburn
Pullen Church Workshop
Raleigh, North Carolina

Yellow
      is like
Seeing little elves
Touching thread
Smelling a flower
Tasting lemon pudding
Hearing someone scream.

Cathy Cates
Aldert Root Elementary School
Raleigh, North Carolina

Later, we use color alone.

A COLOR LIKE ME

A color like me has a sound like me.
I spell you out like Love.
      And the love will be you and me.
            Carry me, carry me.
And I will spell you out.

Mike O'Hara
Aldert Root Elementary School
Raleigh, North Carolina

PURPLE

Purple is like when you can't find
your clothes in the morning and
your mom is sleeping and you put
on some short pants in the winter
and when you get to school
your lunch money is stuck in your
pocket with bubble gum.

Grady Cooper
J.W. York Elementary School
Raleigh, North Carolina

The third day we might use sounds and comparisons together or I might give them a word and have them write three lines about it and then everybody tries to guess what it is. Then, we'll talk about animals and maybe write about animals.

(Sounds)

THUNDER

Thunder is a scary sound;
It makes me feel bad.
Thunder sounds like the
whole earth is breaking
into many pieces.

Martha Cockrell
J.W. York Elementary School
Raleigh, North Carolina

(Animals)

Last night I had a dream,
It was about a horse that I had got.
The color of it is black,
It feels very soft,
And it doesn't make a sound.

Sharon Walker
Guy B. Teachy Elementary School
Asheboro, North Carolina

98

The fourth day, I'll bring pictures from magazines; photo magazines always have some interesting pictures in them. I will also bring objects from home. I'll wander around getting together things like tea strainers, pot holders, small trucks, socks, and so on. I put them, all in a bag and dump them on some table in the room for the kids to rummage through. They might try to write from inside one of the pictures or one of the objects may appeal to them enough to "turn into" it and write as if they were that object.

TOES

Toes come in all shapes and sizes,
They are fat and skinny, long and short.

In the winter they snuggle together in warm wool socks,
In the summer, they expose themselves.

They wiggle and tickle and kick in the sand.
At night, they are still and warm, feeling content,
Under the thick blankets.

Kathy Turnage
Harnett Middle School
Dunn, North Carolina

A SHOE

A shoe is like a person with a
        big, bragging mouth,
It has a tongue that hangs lazily
        around and is a heel when it brags
        too much.
It loses all color when it plays
        too rough.

Todd Boyd
Harnett Middle School
Dunn, North Carolina

The last day I'll have them write about whatever they want to, but try to get them to write with the tools I've already provided.

It's high tide now.
The tides are coming in.
The waves are high as mountain sides
Drifting in the wind.

Jeff Baker
J.W. York Elementary School
Raleigh, North Carolina

DAWN

The sun rises slowly
   like melting gold.
The waters are like
   the softness of chiffon
   the color of aqua.
It sparkles like diamonds
   as the gentle waves splash
   against the sandy banks.

Cindy Strickland
Harnett Middle School
Dunn, North Carolina

During the week I use the things I have learned from previous experiences, like telling them that they can't use each other's name or the teacher's name in the poems. That way lies disaster. I found that out the hard way in the first elementary school I ever went into. I also break up the class hour in the middle by having "fidget time." I tell everyone to stand up and fidget about however they want. Nobody of course knows what fidget means so I have to demonstrate. Soon you have a roomful of wiggly worms. Then we sit down and back to work. I have found that if there's time left over at the end of a class period the kids love to read their work into a tape recorder and then have me play it back. It's a good way to spend a few minutes. It would be better if the teachers could do this after I leave the class for the day, and some of them do, after they discover the way it soothes the savage beasties. Another trick I use is to get them to nominate each other to read when the volunteering breaks down. This way the ones who really want to read, but are embarrassed, get to read, because, after all, if someone nominates you to do something, you really should do it.

About reading the poems . . . kids like to share their work and I try if humanly possible to let them. Sometimes I'll let only those who are actively about to tear down the joint read and sometimes I leave and let the teacher oversee the reading after I've left. On some days when they finish in a great hurry I'll hear all of them. So this fluctuates, but I believe strongly that someone should be available to hear what a student has written.

All of what I have written about the lower grades sounds a lot like what everybody else is doing and it is. However, I have found that these things work and set the stage for whatever comes next, whether it's total abandonment or further nurturing.

From what I can tell, we are all using variations on similar themes. The elementary schools are full of color, sound, comparison, interesting words, collaborations, objects, animals, music and pictures but every poet is using his own way to get results. When the junior and senior highs come into the picture that's where the approach begins to get more diverse and the poems get different.

In the fifth and sixth grades, I work in very similar patterns as in the lower grades. But I spend only one or two days on things like color, sound and comparison. I spend much more time on the use of words and setting up poems on the page and original thoughts. The five senses come separate from the idea of color at this point and I have them mix up the senses without using a color to start off with.

The smell of tar...

> is like the taste of castor oil
> the touch of chewed bubble gum or soggy cereal
> hearing that superman forgot his blue tights
> seeing a rock fall off the cliff and breaking its neck.

Gregory Smith
P.S. Jones Jr. High School
Washington, North Carolina

Tasting a raw oyster...

> is like hearing muddy water drip
> seeing a slimy slug
> smelling a dead fish, and
> touching a bowl of jello with whipped cream

Jane Roebuck
P.S. Jones Jr. High School
Washington, North Carolina

Hearing the waves crash on the rocks is like seeing the clouds roll
through the sky, is like smelling the salt air
    on a warm windy day, is
like touching a pine cone and like
    tasting a hamburger cooked outside.

Karen Holland
P.S. Jones Jr. High School
Washington, North Carolina

One of my favorite things to do is to concentrate on what I call
"good words." I read them a number of poems and ask them to
pick out the good words, interesting words, words that appeal to
them. I commonly read Cam Reeves' poem about the "Dappled Ponies."

THE DAPPLED PONIES

When dappled ponies gobbled roses from the hedges
and cobwebs hung spread-eagled from the wires
dew-clotted innocent of victim bait or spider

When morning ran the mists out of the valley
and all the little suns were coming up at once

    over the mountain

Then I remember steam from kneeling cattle
rising in mushroom puffs above their heads
the fierce horns the sweet and holy haloes
the heavy beasts all born again

    reincarnated saints

Saint Angus and Saint Brahmin
a bull named Gabriel rose like a martyr
a wreath of tenderness around his head

    and knelt again sighing

Saints live long but dew is swift in drying

If grace is sought I think about the valley
nurturing its nectarines and honey
the ponies nibbling roses from the hedges

The dappled ponies with their saddles squeaking.

Campbell Reeves

They can pick out the words I'm talking about even when they don't always understand the words. Then I might read John Ratti's poem "The Market Man" and have them pick out the colors and the senses as well as the good words.

THE MARKET MAN

The walnut brains thing moist
in their light tan skulls;
the apples croon redly
of their tooth white pulp;
and the squash curves voluptuously
in its yellow skin.
It is cold and the market man
burns an orange crate;
It is dark and bare bulbs hang down
like fiery glass pears.
The market man has big blunt thumbs,
he feels chapped melons;
the market man has a strong mouth,
dry as potato dust;
the market man has black grape eyes,
no seeds show in them.
The market man has lonely shanks,
he splats lemons against a wall;
the market man is angry at the cold,
he strips the heads of lettuce down
and throws the green leaves on the cobble street;
the market man smells the salty river,
he bites an onion open with his teeth
and floods the black night with tears and burning.

John Ratti

When I have ascertained that they know what I'm talking about then I have them work with poems of their own, using as many good words as they can think up or find. They will often use the dictionaries to find words. Here the only restriction I have is that they be able to tell me the meaning of any word they use in a poem. Now that doesn't mean that they have to use the word in context, just that they must realize that they are using it out of context if they do. Many interesting poems have come out of this.

(Made-up words)

A SNOWLY WORLD

It's an opaque, snowly world outside,
With ginomenous flakes all over.
It snows beneath the blackened skies,
And the melted flakes are gushey.

I go outside in the frozolden weather,
But it's just for a secment.
I slosh and goush, and muddle in snow,
Until I get too yucky, mucky, uck.

I come inside and drip mucky sluck,
And shiver like a drat.
I drop my snicey outer clothing
And say it was superlishous.

George Runion
P.S. Jones Jr. High School
Washington, North Carolina

(Description of one word)

APPALACHIAN

The word Appalachian
Sounds like tinkling slivers of broken glass,
A hundred tiny clashing cymbals being played by elves,
A million tiny Chinese gongs.

It sounds like the rain,
Falling ever so quietly on the brilliant green leaves
Of the forest.

It is as quiet as marshmallows,
Falling on a cotton floor,
Or the opening of a well-oiled door.

Alan Crawford
P.S. Jones Jr. High School
Washington, North Carolina

(Using good words)

MY SECRET GARDEN

I love to smell the flowers in my secret garden,
    the dew on them in the early morning glow
    is like a rainfall in Bermuda.
The black spider spins her web among the weeds.
The water can is a rough rusty brown.
The trees sway in the cool pleasant breeze.
The army ants march in a steady one, two, one, two.
I love the flashy red in a
    varicolored tomato—
The velocipede left overnight in the rain
    is like a lonely child.

My garden is all to myself.
No one knows about it because
My garden is in me.

Jon Courie
E.C. Brooks Elementary School
Raleigh, North Carolina

AN AFFIRMATION ALABASTER

is a formation with a long
white tail with a head like an ape.
It looks like a zebra because of its stripes,
and has a hump on its back.
His eyes are as big as his wriggly hands.
Its horns are like an elk, and
it has a mouth big as a tuba.
He can hear a hundred yards away,
because his ears have holes all the way through his head.

William Winters
E.C. Brooks Elementary School
Raleigh, North Carolina

WEEPING WILLOW

A Weeping Willow is like a gloomy day.
Or the humonguous empty mist of the sea.
A Weeping Willow reminds me of an old humbug drying in maize.
The rust colored tree cries in the wind with a silent whisper.
The frost wind hits my tongue when I try to say Weeping Willow
    it feels like a tongue twister.
I distrust the squeaking creaking of the rocking tree.
The tree looks like a hairy goon in the fog.
The Willow's moss feels like the cold blood of murder.

Blair Johnson
Aldert Root Elementary School
Raleigh, North Carolina

GARFUNKEL

The word garfunkel sounds like
    a purple snout of a hippopotamus.

Or the weird looking snorkel of
    an elephant.
Or salmon splattering all over
    a muddy river.

Or an octopus gulping seaweed.

There are a lot of things garfunkel
    could be.

Barry Holem
Aldert Root Elementary School
Raleigh, North Carolina

On occasion if a class is having great difficulty adjusting to the good word idea I'll have them do what Koch calls a "jewel box" poem or what I call "the grand scene." You write on the board (with the students' help) lists of things that are interesting, like all the woods, jewels, materials, metals, flowers, birds and so forth that you can think of. Then they fashion a grand scene with these words. The student who has been having difficulty up to this point might just take off with these words spelled and all up before his eyes.

MY SECRET PLACE

Where the maple leaves are a velvet
    brown as they glisten in the sunlight.
Where the wind sweeps over the golden
    wheat.
And the waters sparkling with white and
    blue sparkles.
And the fires sparkling with silver
    and gold.
And the stars glistening with bright
    colored silk.
And the wind whips the clouds around
    wildly as if they were in a mixing
    bowl.
This is the place I love to be as I
    sit in the wind by the old oak tree.

Charlie King
Aldert Root Elementary School
Raleigh, North Carolina

Different ideas have different results with different kids and different classes and schools. I try to have lots of things in my mind at all times so that if one thing seems to be lagging I can use something else. I read all the poems every night that my students do every day so that I can decide what would be the best direction to take the next day with that particular class. That way I can also see which students need more help where and which ones I could be giving more advanced ideas.

One idea that I had is evidently one that a lot of other poets had because I've seen a lot about it in the past few years. I had heard the very alluring fascinating recording of the "Songs of the Humpback Whales" a number of years back as the backdrop of an improvization jazz night at a local college. It had stayed in my mind as a possibility for poetry inspiration. Finally I decided to use the record in a fourth grade class to see if I could get them more interested in the real lives of animals, which are far more fascinating than the pretend works they find in many of their books. This in turn might make them write more realistically about animals. I'd about had my fill of fuzzy ducks, and the terribly romanticized notions kids had about animals. So I played with great relish the recording and we talked about mystery and the real world and then as I played it again I had them write about any animal they wanted to. More fuzzy ducks!

I still had faith in the idea so I used it again the next day with fifth graders. Maybe with their beginning cynicism and their attention to gory detail, I could get them to use the idea successfully. More fuzzy ducks.

Never saying die on this I finally sat and thought and thought about how I (obviously it had to be my fault with such a superb notion at my fingertips) was goofing up. It came in a flash that I was ignoring the word "song" in my efforts to get across the animal idea. The next week I was in a middle school where I played the record and had the students think about the strange under-sea world and indeed the strange world of any place where we didn't live and the animals did. And if you were to write a song of yourself what would it say? If you were a tree and you were writing a song of yourself what would you say. At last I got some good work, but not on animals necessarily. Which goes to show that most good ideas will work but not always the way you want them to or with the age group you had in mind.

THE WHALE

A whale glides gently over the sea,
Oh what fun, what fun that must be,
Tossing and turning, he leaps through the air,
You'd think he didn't have one little care.
The sun falls slowly among the clouds,
The sound of the whales is lingering out.

Alan Jones
Harnett Middle School
Dunn, North Carolina

A SONG OF THE WIND

Howling on a rainy night,
Ruffling clothes on a line
    in mid-day sunshine,
Blowing through grass in a
    tall wheat field,
Alone, all alone.

Singing through bushes in the
    yard at evening.

Flowing through a small boy's
    hair as he runs in delight.
Warm, gently blowing on a
    summer's night,
Alone, all alone.

It's good to be the wind,
And sing all day,
But when the winter ends,
I just blow away
Alone, all alone.

Lee Faircloth
Harnett Middle School
Dunn, North Carolina

The worst thing about this whole idea is trying to get a copy of the record. I called the record stores in our area and had the devil's own time trying to convince them that the Humpback Whales weren't a singing group. I'd hear someone in the background asking, "Is it a kid on the phone?" Finally I had to track down the person who owned the record that was used in the program I'd heard, and then borrow it. Keep it for a while I was told, it's not something we play for dinner music every night.

The fifth and sixth grades are beginning to care more about form and how to set up the lines of their poems. Of course there's no way to really teach that. But I can use an overhead projector or mimeographed poems where we can look and see what other poets have done. But then I can't say for sure to them why some of the line breaks and punctuation are as they are; only the poets know that for sure and maybe even they have forgotten by now. But it gives the kids a chance to see what others have done and to know that they can do pretty much what they want to do if it's consistent.

Back a few years ago when I was trying to get some ideas about how to go out and conquer the poetry teaching business I heard about the idea of found poems. Now in this genre you are supposed to, or the kids are supposed to, cut strips of words out of the newspaper and put various strips back together to form "found poems." Somehow I didn't get that too well and thought the kids were supposed to do something more like make posters out of words cut out of the newspaper. So I came into a sixth grade one day with lots of poster paper and lots of newspapers, glue, and scissors and the kids went wild fixing their word posters. I think it's a good fun thing to do in the middle of the week, and I do it occasionally, although I no longer call it "found." The way the room looks after they're through it would be more like "lost." In any case that's what can happen with an idea gone astray.

When you are working in a school for five days straight and out of town, it's ridiculous to assume that all the poems from the day before are going to be all typed up to use in the classroom the next day. For one thing the logistics are unreal. How can someone be working all night typing up the poems with an eye toward running them off at dawn on some school's mimeo machine while at the same time I am supposed to be reading them and editing or making comments or trying to decide what to do the next day. Not even poems can be in two places at the same time. So I believe the best thing to hope for is an anthology of the poems which has a poem by every child in the program to come out as soon as possible after your departure. The way to let the kids have exposure while you're there is to let them read the poems in class.

I've been using something recently, however, which works very well to give the students instant publication. The best way I've found to do this is to get the principal to designate one well-traveled hall wall as the poetry publication wall and to supply you with a very large roll of masking tape, lots of colored construction paper, glue, scissors, and several boxes of all different colored felt tipped pens. At most schools, it is good to prepare in advance. It's amazing how difficult it can be to requisition a large roll of masking tape and a few dozen felt tipped pens.

What you do is let the kids choose anything they write to go on the board. They then choose the color paper they want, cut it in any design that turns them on, copy the poem on it with aforementioned pens, and mask it to the wall to be read and admired (and sometimes stolen) by schoolmates, passing parents, teachers, and other personnel. They may or may not want to put their names on these works of art.

In addition to instant publication, this affords the students an opportunity to take a good look at what they've written and to tidy up or change their work if necessary. Also, it gives them some association with the color and the physical shape of the poem they have written.

This takes either a period of your time or some of the teachers' time or both, but it is certainly worth it and can be a big selling point for the parents when they come into the school and see some of their kids' work. In many cases, I know that the anthologies go home and nobody pays them much attention, but if the poetry is on the wall in living color, it's hard to miss.

I like working with all ages. The little ones are refreshing with their affection, admiration, and all-out imaginations. The middle grades, fifth and sixth, make me feel young again with their antics, jokes, and last flings before becoming big junior highs. But the junior and senior highs make me work like I've never worked before. It takes so much more effort on my part because they are so serious about what they're doing. I honestly don't know what I'm going to do from one day to the next or from one class to the next. They go off on different tangents and levels and they all have such different needs.

In the junior high I work more with suggesting things to do and with the senior high I do more just throwing things and ideas and poems out to them and see what catches hold. I do have a "first day spiel" however which I use to impart information and which also has enough holes in it to allow me and the students some opportunity for conversation and establishing rapport. It goes something like this:

I tell them my name and write it in the corner of the board. Kimzey is not your everyday name and even acquaintances forget it until they've seen it spelled or heard it a number of times. This avoids my telling the kids my name fifty times the first day and even thereafter. We discuss the facts which I throw out to them such as there will be no grades and no push to provide me with a poem every day or at all, but that they'll have more fun if they'll give it a try. Most of them know that there's going to be an anthology at the end of the program. The teachers seem to get that across when nothing else sinks in. For that reason alone most of them do write. If after the first two days I realize that someone's not writing, I'll drift over and try to find out why. Usually, this doesn't happen if there's a degree of discipline in the room.

Speaking of discipline I'll digress just a moment to address myself to this knotty problem. I have seen a class of the most well-behaved sophomores one could hope for dissolve into a morass of misconduct when the teacher steps out of the room. It's as if all the frustrations at the school's system pop out the minute the boss disappears. If you're in that classroom I don't care how well you think you can handle students of all ages there is certainly a bit of panic at that moment. There are many programs in other states that will not put a poet into the classroom without a teacher present. They claim, and for good reason, that the program is intended to train teachers too, and so it is. However for all practical purposes, in some cases the teachers just aren't around. I suppose in this state we have coddled our schools because we knew that in some if we required the teachers to be present the school wouldn't have the program. That is probably paranoid and inaccurate. But most of the requests come from teachers or superintendents and not always with the principals' blessing. Of course any combination of this can occur like principal and superintendent and not teachers, etc. But where the principal is not totally dedicated to what you're doing he's going to be reluctant to excuse teachers from classes and pay for a substitute out of school funds.

Most schools put together these poetry classes outside of regular classes and so the teacher is expected to stay with her regular class. For him or her to leave or for many to leave, someone has to fill their spot. This costs money, and/or time for the rest of the students. Even though you point out that it's only for one week many are not willing to go that mile. So you are left with this class of kids you've never seen before and they've never seen you before and you don't know which ones are the troublemakers and which ones are the leaders or anything. Of course this emerges quickly and you have to watch more for that sort of thing the first few days. I don't mind teaching without a teacher present unless things get really out of hand at the beginning. (This usually happens when the kids have no other time during the day to talk or kid around with each other.) Then I'll call in a teacher. Strangely enough a principal will release a teacher quicker to keep order than to learn something about the poetry process. They don't care about the teacher learning something but by all that's mighty they're not going to be embarrassed in front of an outsider by their kids raising hell.

Back to the first day, we discuss things like spelling and line breaks and I assure them that that doesn't matter for now and when it does I'll let them know and help them with it. I will talk to them some about proper subjects for poetry — that is, there aren't any. To pursue this I might read them the table of contents of an anthology like *Some Haystacks Don't Even Have Any Needle*. The titles of the poems in that anthology happen to be particularly unusual, although I imagine any contemporary anthology would do. We talk about rhyme and I use most of the Koch arguments against it, like creating backwards, the likelihood of saying the same thing over and over, and the possibility of getting silly where you don't want to. Most of this I cover lightly because these kids are the age to know most of that and they don't rhyme anyway. I do want to stake myself out from the beginning however. I also talk about the repetition of words and phrases and sounds to use instead of rhyme.

We talk about color and sound and comparisons and the five senses, but I no longer have them do any of the exercise work that I have the younger students do. They'd rather have you talk about it and let them kibitz and then listen to some of the poems others have written that are in the student anthologies. They really like sharing what the younger ones have written even though they don't want to do the things themselves.

This usually ends up the first day. I do tell them that if any of them have poems already written that they'd like me to take a look at I'll be around all week and will be happy to see them.

What happens from then on is entirely up for grabs. Any number of ways of working might appeal to me the next day. And what I want to do might bomb with them so I have many ideas and things to do available with me. The following are some of the things I might have on tap.

One of the ways I always like to work is by example. As I come across a poem in my reading during the year that I think I might want to use in a class sometime I try to xerox it out or have it typed up. So I keep a large envelope of poems to pull from. In some schools where aides are available, I try to get them to run off master sheets of poems I want to work with or want the kids to be able to see while we're talking about them.

Some days we'll take these poems and divide them up and I'll divide the kids up into groups and let them sit around in corners or wherever they want to gather away from the others. Then someone in the group reads the poems and they decide which one they like the best. And always there have to be some reasons. We get back together as a class and someone reads their group's choice and tells why they like it. It can be for very simple reasons, but I need to know that they read it at least. This serves the purpose of having them hear and see contemporary poetry and to think it over without benefit of my judgment, except of course I chose the poems in the first place.

I don't come in the first day with my own poems in hand ready to read them. I know some poets do and with very good results and the kids love it and don't think they're full of conceit and pomp. But I can't do that; it isn't my nature and I feel awkward about it. I know that it's a good way for the kids to know you and what you're thinking but I still can't do it right then. I try to let them know me in other ways. If they start asking however and then get persistent beyond mere nice manners then I do bring in a few poems I think they might enjoy. At that point they do loosen up with me much more and I with them. There's not an audience in the world that wants to be read poetry forever. So I read until I feel that they're beginning to get restless and then I stop. Some students don't even ask you about your work and in that case I don't lay it on them. I figure the teacher read it to them before I came and that was enough, or they know I write poetry but they're more interested in kidding around with me and getting to know me that way. So any way is all right.

I use the same number of slides and pictures that most everybody else does. I don't get the uniform quality with slides that some poets do, nor do I get special results with pictures although I always have them around. Maybe it's because I've never seen the end result being anything I could hang my hat on and that makes me personally feel incomplete about that way of working. On the other hand, I have seen poems done by kids with slide and picture inspiration that were knockouts. I suspect that it depends on how the individual approaches the whole matter. Once we had a set of slides that were nothing but different kinds of doors. A friend of mine had done them as part of some project he was working on and I asked him if I might borrow them to have three sets made for use in our program. I sent out the word that I had them in the office the year I ran the program and a few poets were interested enough to send in for them and to use them in their classrooms. They had all kinds of poems about doors and those with the slides brought forth some interesting responses. That's the kind of thing that folks use every now and then to break the monotony.

The day I tried to use the door slides we couldn't get the room dark enough to show them to advantage. The kids were restless and it was hot in the school and they were eighth graders and it was spring. So they begged to go outside and write. Let us go through the door, pleeeeze Miz. K. So we did ramble out and right over to a cemetery next to the school and they sat around and wrote cemetery and dead poems and had a much better experience than if I'd insisted on staying to fight the doors.

I'm forever trying to get the kids to write about something they've never written about before. Music sometimes breaks down this barrier. I have lots of poet teachers tell me that dreams are the key to this but somehow I've never had much luck with them. I have had luck

114

with a type of mind-letting-go weird music writing. Two of the pieces I use are "Ionization" by Varese from *Sounds of New Music* (Folkways) and "Ensembles for Synthesizer," by Milton Babbitt, from the album *New Electronic Music* from Leaders of the Avant-Garde. I'm sure there are many more, especially now, but something they can't put a form to is good. In playing classical music I found that some tuned it out and those who didn't all heard the same things. So the shaped-up pieces really don't work too well unless you have a topic in mind and you're trying to match it with music.

(Writing to music)

TRIPPING OUT

The junkie's pad is ready to trip out to a world beyond.
Nets, lights & black posters, pipes, incense, roaches,
psychedelic lights, and even that cloud of evil smoke
that take the mind and winds it up into little balls,
hammering it, sticking needles in it, protruding
into each nerve and vein to send the mind into a trance.

A match is lit to that roll of seeds that taste so good,
    so good.
That fragrance of sweet-smelling smoke that is inhaled,
down, down, deep in the lungs.
The junkie & the pusher sit and stare endlessly
still sipping on the lit jay.

Get high, man! Get high!
No, but the nickel bag wasn't enough.
Got's to have the needle.
He's strung out, strung out, need that needle to pop that
acid in the main vein.
Got to have that coke, and that LSD—little sip of dope.

Now you're flying—high, high, higher, highest.
Your mind is in a constant flaming and it's deteriorating
each moment.
It spins in an endless stop, never ceasing whirlpool.

You got that high, but D-O-P-E says
Kill, Kill, Kill
Die, Die, Die.

And a life has been wasted in a world that never was.

Randy Coan
Salisbury High School
Salisbury, N.C.

First and last lines given to them sometimes work, but often they just sit and look at them and can't get their own thoughts going in the right directions. Something I like better is free association. You read them a poem and they write down all kinds of words that pop into their minds, not using any of the words in the poem. Then they use the words they like the best in a poem of their own. One particular day I was using James Wright's "A Blessing" and one of the students wrote a free association poem from it.

A BLESSING

Just off the highway to Rochester, Minnesota,
Twilight bounds softly forth on the grass.
And the eyes of those two Indian ponies
Darken with kindness.
They have come gladly out of the willows
To welcome my friend and me.
We step over the barbed wire into the pasture
Where they have been grazing all day, alone.
They ripple tensely, they can hardly contain their happiness
That we have come.
They bow shyly as wet swans. They love each other.
There is no loneliness like theirs.
At home once more,
They begin munching the young tufts of spring in the darkness.
I would like to hold the slenderer one in my arms,
For she has walked over to me
And nuzzled my left hand.
She is black and white,
Her mane falls wild on her forehead,
And the light breeze moves me to caress her long ear
That is delicate as the skin over a girl's wrist.

116

Suddenly I realize
That if I stepped out of my body I would break
Into blossom.

James Wright

(Free Association from Wright poem)

FLOWERPONY

flowerpony nuzzles
   cold fingers
nostrils sniffing
   sniffing i smile

barnwind on the hood
   of the pickup
lonely scrubgrass
   wavering i shudder

prairiepine in clear
   cloudysun horizon
on blossomneedles
   resting i sleep

Jerry Saucier
Sanderson High School
Raleigh, N.C.

On a slow day it's sometimes fun to do some mimic poems. By a slow day I mean one where the kids have been writing well and hard for a few days and they're kind of written out for the time being. The two I like to use the best are "Thirteen Ways of Looking at a Blackbird" by Wallace Stevens, and "Things To Do Around A Lookout" by Gary Snyder. In "Thirteen Ways" they usually can't understand the entire poem but at least get the idea that we're talking about turning a thing every way but loose, and looking at it and recording our observations all the while. With the "Lookout" poem they're seeing that sometimes if you use lists of things in a proper sequence and with proper undertones you can fashion a poem. Cummings' poems are also fun to work with.

(Stevens imitation)

WAYS TO FALL OUT OF A WINDOW

To be pushed by an elephant.
   To be scared by a fly.
Being pushed by a bulldozer.
     Accidently slipping on a
     banana peeling.
By seeing visions of girls dancing
through the sky.
     To go to sleep thinking about
     your true love.
To be struck by a tiger's paw.
     Reaching for a note and slipping.
Just to get carried away and fall
       down
          down
             down.

Terry Pope
Harnett Elementary School
Dunn, N.C.

(Cummings imitation)

Butterflyflute heard a lullabyinsky
In a beautiful tone.
Summerdaylike today was magicwonderful
And birdyneat was laughjumping all at once.
Satywoodpecker was scumming on a lumshistree.
Momyweakadeer was eating a deliciousmunshus patch
Of strawberriesan.
Oh me, it is a cooleeday.

Nicole Pediaditakis
J. W. York Elementary School
Raleigh, North Carolina

Another slow day idea that works for me is the word box. I tried all different kinds of ways working with individual words and like this best. I write down about three hundred words and then cut them out and put them in the "word box." Then the kids draw out six.

They must use these six to shape a poem, a news release, a story, an advertisement, or whatever they wish, but they must use all six words. They may have more if they want but they must use them and there's no swapping off with friends or with me. The words are always funny or far out or strange or something special and the students really have a lot of fun with them, all the while learning that it sometimes works out quite well to put strange combinations of words together. The words one might pull could include some like this: fox, taffeta, hamburger, stomp, Elton John, and sissy.

As the week progresses one of the major problems is not in eliminating rhyme or meter, but in getting rid of abstractions. I pull out an exercise I use in trying to quietly bring their use of abstractions to their attention. We discuss what an abstraction is and that the opposite of abstract is concrete. I talk to them about trying to tie down their feelings a bit more. Then together we put some abstractions on the board such as love, hate, loneliness, happiness, sadness, and so on. (Some editor, at Teachers and Writers Collaborative as a matter of fact, told me I was making a mistake to limit the abstractions to feelings, but should add things like civilization, honesty, honor, etc. I tried that, but the kids preferred, as I had figured they would, love, hate, etc.) Then we make a list of funny words like tennis shoes, the porch swing, spaghetti, or light bulb. I ask them to compare an abstract word with a concrete word and tell why it's alike and in doing so make the whole effort into a kind of poem. Of course they make up their own lists to work with and some write only a few lines and some a whole page.

> Love is like a lamp,
> You can turn it on or off.
> Loneliness is like a chair,
> They both sit still with nothing to do.
> Happiness is like my big toe,
> If you step on it too hard you might
>   break it.

Guilt is like mud,
They both make you feel dirty.
Sorrow is like grass,
It can flow in a different direction
    or it can stay the same.

Glenda Mackie
Aldert Root School
Raleigh, N. C.

Hate is like bushes between houses
because they separate people.

Love is like a school
because you learn from it.

Friendship is like a sucker
because if you don't bite it, it lasts a long time.

Fil Stidham
P.S. Jones Jr. High School
Washington, N.C.

Love is like paper,
paper can be shredded and so can a heart.

Envy is like a grocery tape,
you add it all up and it can cost you.

Life is like spaghetti,
It's nothing without the meatballs.

Grief is like a fishing rod,
cast it out too far and it's hard to get back in.

War is like a typewriter,
push the wrong key and it's hard to erase.

Friendship is like a bag,
blow it up, push it too far and it bursts.

Hate is like mud,
keep it up and it gets to be a messy game.

Doogie Hodges
P.S. Jones Jr. High School
Washington, N.C.

After this I can say to them, could you be more concrete in this line or in this poem and they at least know what I mean, whether they choose to do it or not. After one such talk as this I got a great love poem from one of the girls who obviously had real talent, but who was wasting it on an every-day-affair love, love, love, poem. I said, can you write about love without using the word, and she could. This is something that takes about fifteen minutes all together and is fun and gets the message across. I also read them the love and loneliness poems in the anthology and they can see how their contemporaries have dealt with feelings in a clear and untrite way.

Laughing in slow motion
Sunlight in our tea
Holding hands and nothing more
As the sun slides below the world.

Sleeping in the grass with the sun
Examining our faces
You're the nicest thing anyone has
          ever given me.

Sally Lomax
Salisbury High School
Salisbury, N.C.

TO SHELLEY

A sword has entered my back and
          pierced your beautiful body.
We walked together, sword between us.
Through reynolda and time the sword
          moved deeper.

121

Unreachable the lance was us.
Now . . . it has removed.
The opening.
    The opening.

Dennis Thaw
Salisbury High School
Salisbury, N.C.

REFLECTIONS OF ME

Reflected—
The broken light
of a glass pond
to my eyes.
I see me.
I touch me.
I break me.
Yearning and fearing
touch, itself.
By a hope? a hand? a love?

Dana Sturm
Sanderson High School
Raleigh, N.C.

The part of the week's program that I think does the most good, however, comes from their hearing poems, poems and more poems. You can almost see their "ears" developing for contemporary sounds. I have two things in mind about this way of working. One is the ideas and concepts set forth in Ted Hughes' *Poetry Is*. Here he groups poetry around certain things, places, people, or ideas. From this I have devised my own list of poems under the headings of images, places, feelings, philosophies, narratives, humor, sports, people, animals, objects and things. In addition to this list, I have individual poems which I use to get across certain other aspects of poetry. I believe the use of these in the context of the ideas behind poems is a successful way to work in senior high schools.

122

Of course images are everywhere but I like to use the poem "Wuthering Heights" by Sylvia Plath from Hughes' book. Also any self-respecting haiku will do the trick, although I personally don't use them.

WUTHERING HEIGHTS

The horizons ring me like faggots,
Tilted and disparate, and always unstable.
Touched by a match, they might warm me,
And their fine lines singe
The air to orange
Before the distances they pin evaporate,
Weighting the pale sky with a solider colour.
But they only dissolve and dissolve
Like a series of promises, as I step forward.

There is no life higher than the grasstops
Or the hearts of sheep, and the wind
Pours by like destiny, bending
Everything in one direction.
I can feel it trying
To funnel my heat away.
If I pay the roots of the heather
Too close attention, they will invite me
To whiten my bones among them.

The sheep know where they are,
Browsing in their dirty wool-clouds,
Grey as the weather,
The black slots of their pupils take me in.
It is like being mailed into space,
A thin silly message.
They stand about in grandmotherly disguise,
All wig curls and yellow teeth
And hard, marbly baas.

I come to wheel ruts and water
Limpid as the solitudes
That flee through my fingers.
Hollow doorsteps go from grass to grass;

Lintel and sill have unhinged themselves.
Of people the air only
Remembers a few odd syllables.
It rehearses them moaningly:
Black stone, black stone.

The sky leans on me, me, the one upright
Among all horizontals.
The grass is beating its head distractedly.
It is too delicate
For a life in such company;
Darkness terrifies it.
Now, in valleys narrow
And black as purses, the house lights
Gleam like small change.

Sylvia Plath

One idea I like is using objects to evoke emotion. Poems like "Stone" and "Summer Morning" by Charles Simic are excellent examples of this. Also I like the simplicity of "Vase: September" by Gary Snyder.

STONE

Go inside a stone
That would be my way.
Let somebody else become a dove
Or gnash with a tiger's tooth.
I am happy to be a stone.

From the outside the stone is a riddle:
No one knows how to answer it.
Yet within, it must be cool and quiet
Even though a cow steps on it full weight,
Even though a child throws it in a river;
The stone sinks, slow, unperturbed
To the river bottom
Where the fishes come to knock on it
And listen.

I have seen sparks fly out
When two stones are rubbed,
So perhaps it is not dark inside after all;
Perhaps there is a moon shining
From somewhere, as though behind a hill—
Just enough light to make out
The strange writings, the star-charts
On the inner walls.

Charles Simic

SUMMER MORNING

I love to stretch
Like this, naked
On my bed in the morning;
Quiet, listening:

Outside they are opening
Their primers
In the little school
Of the cornfield.

There is a smell of damp hay.
Of horses, of summer sky,
Of laziness, of eternal life.

I know all the dark places
Where the sun hasn't reached yet,
Where the singing has just ceased
In the hidden aviaries of the crickets—
Anthills where it goes on raining—
Slumbering spiders dreaming of wedding dresses.

I pass over the farmhouses
Where the little mouths open to suck,
Barnyards where a man, naked to the waist,
Washes his face with a hose,
Where the dishes begin to rattle in the kitchen.

The good tree with its voice
Of a mountain brook
Knows my steps
It hushes.

I stop and listen:
Somewhere close by
A stone cracks a knuckle,
Another turns over in its sleep.

I hear a butterfly stirring
In the tiny soul of the caterpillar.
I hear the dust dreaming
Of eyes and great winds.

Further ahead, someone
Even more silent
Passes over the grass
Without bending it,

—And all of a sudden
In the midst of that silence
It seems possible
To live simply
On the earth.

Charles Simic

VASE: SEPTEMBER

Old Mrs. Kawabata
cuts down the tall spike weeds—
    more in two hours
than I can get done in a day.
Out of a mountain
of grass and thistle
she saved five dusty stalks
    of ragged wild blue flower
and put them in my kitchen in a jar.

Gary Snyder

And nowhere is there a narrative like "Cherrylog Road" (too long to quote here) by James Dickey to get to students. They love it without reservation. Another of his poems, "The Heaven of Animals," is an excellent animal poem to share that shuns romanticism and sets a good example.

THE HEAVEN OF ANIMALS

Here they are. The soft eyes open.
If they have lived in a wood
It is a wood.
If they have lived on plains
It is grass rolling
Under their feet forever.

Having no souls, they have come,
Anyway, beyond their knowing.
Their instincts wholly bloom
And they rise.
The soft eyes open.

To match them, the landscape flowers,
Outdoing, desperately
Outdoing what is required:
The richest wood,
The deepest field.

For some of these,
It could not be the place
It is, without blood.
These hunt, as they have done,
But with claws and teeth grown perfect,

More deadly than they can believe.
They stalk more silently,
And crouch on the limbs of trees,
And their descent
Upon the bright backs of their prey

May take years
In a sovereign Floating of joy.

And those that are hunted
Know this as their life,
Their reward: to walk

Under such trees in full knowledge
Of what is in glory above them,
And to feel no fear,
But acceptance, compliance.
Fulfilling themselves without pain

At the cycle's center,
They tremble, they walk
Under the tree,
They fall, they are torn,
They rise, they walk again.

James Dickey

Two "have you ever felt this way" poems are "Crow and the Sea" by Ted Hughes and "Something I've Not Done" by W. S. Merwin. At some point everyone there in the room has come up against something they couldn't deal with and had to resolve emotionally. Also everyone can certainly relate to the feeling of the something undone. So these are good poems to show how to deal with everyday occurrences that are universal yet personal.

CROW AND THE SEA

He tried ignoring the sea
But it was bigger than death, just as it was bigger than life.

He tried talking to the sea
But his brain shuttered and his eyes winced from it as from open
flame.

He tried sympathy for the sea
But it shouldered him off—as a dead thing shoulders you off.

He tried hating the sea
But instantly felt like a scrutty dry rabbit dropping on the windy
cliff.

He tried just being in the same world as the sea
But his lungs were not deep enough.

And his cheery blood banged off it
Like a water-drop off a hot stove.

Finally

He turned his back and he marched away from the sea

As a crucified man cannot move.

Ted Hughes

SOMETHING I'VE NOT DONE

Something I've not done
is following me
I haven't done it again and again
so it has many footsteps
like a drumstick that's grown old and never been used

In late afternoon I hear it come closer
at times it climbs out of a sea
onto my shoulders
and I shrug it off
losing one more chance

Every morning
it's drunk up part of my breath for the day
and knows which way
I'm going
and already it's not done there

But once more I say I'll lay hands on it
tomorrow
and add its footsteps to my heart
and its story to my regrets
and its silence to my compass

W. S. Merwin

I like the simple voicing of William Carlos Williams, but am not sure I like using the too simple "This Is Just To Say." Using a poem idea like that is just a fill in the blanks so far as I'm concerned. I'd much rather the students hear something else of his like "The Last Words of My English Grandmother."

THE LAST WORDS OF MY ENGLISH GRANDMOTHER

There were some dirty plates
and a glass of milk
beside her on a small table
near the rank, disheveled bed—

Wrinkled and nearly blind
she lay and snored
rousing with anger in her tones
to cry for food,

Gimme something to eat—
They're starving me—
I'm all right I won't go
to the hospital. No, no, no

Give me something to eat
Let me take you
to the hospital, I said
and after you are well

you can do as you please.
She smiled, Yes
you do what you please first
then I can do what I please—

Oh, oh, oh! she cried
as the ambulance men lifted
her to the stretcher—
Is this what you call

making me comfortable?
By now her mind was clear—
Oh you think you're smart
you young people,

she said, but I'll tell you
you don't know anything.
Then we started.
On the way

We passed a long row
of elms. She looked at them
awhile out of
the ambulance and said,

What are all those
fuzzy-looking things out there?
Trees? Well, I'm tired
of them and rolled her head away.

William Carlos Williams

That also verges on the people angle and I love to use William Stafford's poems about people because he can write about them in such an effective way. The one I use the most often is "Aunt Mabel."

AUNT MABEL

This town is haunted by some good deed
that reappears like a country cousin, or truth
when language falters these days trying to lie,
because Aunt Mabel, an old lady gone now, would
accost even strangers to give bright flowers
away, quick as a striking snake. It's deeds like this
have weakened me, shaken by intermittent trust,
stricken with friendliness.

Our Senator talked like war, and Aunt Mabel
said, "He's a brilliant man,
but we didn't elect him that much."

Everyone's resolve weakens toward evening
or in a flash when a face melds—a stranger's, even—
reminded for an instant between menace and fear:
There are Aunt Mabels all over the world,
    or their graves in the rain.

William Stafford

131

I also like Stafford's "Allegiances" in the life philosophy line. And the puzzle-like poem of Mark Strand's, "Keeping Things Whole," is interesting to the students.

ALLEGIANCES

It is time for all the heroes to go home
if they have any, time for all of us common ones
to locate ourselves by the real things
we live by.

Far to the north, or indeed in any direction,
strange mountains and creatures have always lurked—
elves, goblins, trolls, and spiders:—we
enounter them in dread and wonder.

But once we have tasted far streams, touched the gold,
found some limit beyond the waterfall,
a season changes, and we come back, changed
but safe, quiet, grateful.

Suppose an insane wind holds all the hills
while strange beliefs whine at the traveler's ears,
we ordinary beings can cling to the earth and love
where we are, sturdy for common things.

William Stafford

KEEPING THINGS WHOLE

In a field
I am the absence
of field.
This is
always the case.
Wherever I am
I am what is missing.

When I walk
I part the air

and always
the air moves in
to fill the spaces
where my body's been.

We all have reasons
for moving.
I move
to keep things whole.

                    Mark Strand

One last poem that students really like is Diane Wakoski's
"Thanking My Mother for Piano Lessons." (Too long to quote here.)
There's not a girl in the class who can't use and relate to that lesson
in remembering and belated thanking.

There are of course many more poems which I use. These are
just a few and I don't even have one for each of the above-mentioned
categories, but everybody will have his own favorites or can find just
the right poem for what he's working with. There are listings in the
back mentioning a number of special anthologies, among them those
which are in certain areas like sports and humor.

A special word about humor. I've given up trying to find good
humor poems that don't rhyme, so I simply tell the kids that
obviously funny poems drop right out of the category of no rhyme
and I can't explain it. Funny poems are still those in which part of
their appeal lies in being able to fit them together like a puzzle.

After all is said and done in any of the schools, the anthology
should be the public highlight of the poetry program when everyone
can finally see something of theirs in print. Needless to say, every
student should be consulted about the poem that's going in the
anthology in case they have something against it going out into the
world. This applies mainly to high school and junior high because the
younger students write such volumes and they don't ever seem to care
which of the poems you use just as long as you use one.

The following are examples of student work from some of my schools.

LOST SEASONS

The wind blew
A tree danced
The birds appear
While snow melts
And spring is here.
Everyone's happy
The children play
Adults open windows
And youth is stuck
    lost between seasons.

Karen Long
Salisbury High School
Salisbury, N.C.

UNDERSTAND ME

They ask why? why?
You mean you don't dig on
    my doing.
Yea! I went to the office and
    went home.
I was in that fight at the game
    the other night.
I was the first to walk out when
    we asked them to stop.
No man, all you can do is
    ask why. The reason
later brotherman.

Susong
Salisbury High School
Salisbury, N.C.

MOOD

Night falls like a curtain of black silk,
Wild limbs stretch the sky.
Darkness caresses the earth,
As ghostlike reflections jump forward.
Expectation runs with the breeze,
That whispers of sunrise and broken promises.

Mara Taylor
Sanderson High School
Raleigh, N.C.

STREET GIRL

behind the twilight screen
the girl stands
waiting for hopeful glances

inside the stale dark doorway
she watches
behind the curtains of rain

smudges of fingerprints left inked
        upon glasses
candles drip wax on elegant rugs
purple stockings hang on empty shadows

through open windows
curtains blow
a flower wilts on the table

Becky Copeland
Sanderson High School
Raleigh, N.C.

RINGS IN A BATHTUB

Rings in a bathtub
        like . . .
    Spider-webs
Woven by the oldest of clibberglobs,
        but . . .
    One can escape from
a bathtub.
    Experience will tell,
it's much easier than skiing on
    green
        banana
            peels
Or . . .
    flying
      a
         kite
            with . . .
Soft Spaghetti . . . !

Bobby James
Parkland High School
Winston-Salem, N.C.

RENAISSANCE FAIR

Ladies move through fields of yellow and orange.
Sweetness hides the hard core of pain that
pulses through the silk, nothing hides but
blindness.
Fake, wildly funny, laugh at the organ that
sings calmly of peace.
The jester knows, he is a fat bear rounding
Into the circle. He laughs and jokes.
See the happy jester with the sword in his heart.
Everything at the Fair swirls and flashes to the
lute that is a foghorn. A plane takes
off from the time.

Catherine Brandon
Salisbury High School
Salisbury, N.C.

Cotton cloth
Clothes line smell
Cool ice water days
There's no hurry here.

Music so perfect
Muscles in my mouth twitch
I could dance
A wet grass ballet.

Mandy Lyerly
Salisbury High School
Salisbury, N.C.

I'd like to refer back to the beginning for a moment about the questions involved in teaching poetry, and relate a true story that happened to me just this year. I have been working for two years in a school about an hour's drive from my home in a "Right-to-Read" Program. Last year I was there for 14 days and this year for 21. I spread the days this year over a seven week period. Needless to say, I got to know the kids very well. One of the last days I was there we had a day which wasn't typical, but is one that has stayed in my mind for a number of reasons.

I had a room of my own there and the students came to me at specified times. It was a room on the sixth grade hall, tremendous, with tall ceilings and the enormous windows that are the signature of the older schools in the south. We had long tables in the room with chairs around them and some individual desks for those who preferred them. There was also space on the floor in the corners and near the front if anybody wanted to sit on the floor. The sessions I had with some of the classes were very informal with everybody sitting around on the huge window ledges with their legs half in and half out of the room. Some of the younger ones (I had grades 5-8) there had to sit at the table because with no teachers and heterogeneous groupings they were not quite ready to be able to settle down if sitting in the windows was an option.

I was eating lunch in the teachers' lounge that day when someone came running down the hall to get the principal. Some child seemed to be choking to death on something and nobody could do anything about it. The principal took off at a run and yelled to the secretary to call the rescue squad. The rest of us stood around in the hall and tried to find out what was happening and keep the kids who weren't already in the hall, out of it. The student was in the room across from mine, and I had a class on the way in a few minutes but I figured the other teachers would hold onto their classes. I stepped outside the building when the rescue squad came. By then, several police cars and the sheriff's car were there. I walked over to the policeman and asked how things were going. It appeared that the boy had had some kind of seizure but was breathing again and they thought he'd be all right. They were going to take him to the local hospital until he stabilized and then take him to a larger hospital later in the afternoon. They brought him out to the squad ambulance and I saw the teacher get in with him for the trip to the hospital. They had already called the parents to meet them.

I took off back into the school and to my room because I thought maybe the principal would want me to take the kids from the absent teacher's room into mine until she returned. Also my class was expected momentarily. In the hall there was the chaos I expected with kids crying and praying and nervous and shaky. Death had come a little too close to be just an excitement. It had reached a core in some of the kids. I offered to take some of the ones in the hall in my room but the principal and teachers got it all together and he sent one of the teachers and her class plus the other class out on the playground.

My class came trooping in and they were full of what had happened. They wanted to crowd around me and sit on my desk and at my feet and as close as possible. We moved the desk and tables and we all sat on the floor so everybody could be touching somebody. And we talked about what had happened. So much to talk about and so much to share. We all had been shaken enough to feel very close and share some feelings that we maybe wouldn't have shared before. As it came time for them to leave the intercom came on and someone announced that we had tornado watches in effect and for all teachers to have the halls cleared, rooms ready, and children prepared in the event that a tornado warning went into effect. The watch means that weather conditions are ripe for the spawning of a tornado, and a warning means that one has actually been sighted.

One class left and I still had one to go for the day. During the few minutes I had before the next class came in, I flew down to the office to see what I was supposed to do if a tornado warning was actually announced. I figured the other teachers already knew what to do and I didn't want my class blown away due to my ignorance. Well, we were supposed to raise all the windows about six inches from the bottom, fold the chairs and put them in a pile, and if a warning

138

came we were to get out into the hall and lie flat. I could tell that I wasn't going to be so happy about lying in the hall of that old sixth grade wing with eight other teachers and all those sixth graders. But there was nothing else to do. Tornados are a relatively new occurrence in North Carolina as far as weather conditions are concerned and there weren't too many shelters available.

My students came in the room all a-twitter with the goings on and we put the windows where we were supposed to and got the room in order and I gave them the instructions I had been given. Then we settled down like the other class had; they wanting to sit close also. There are no loners or troublemakers on a day like this one. We talked, about death and fear and tornados and about all kinds of things. It never occurred to me to ask them to write, or to think about leaving them to start home. I only thought about doing one thing at the time. It was like moving through syrup as I look back on that day. All of the fears and worries that they had I had, except I had more information than they did. I knew that the boy would be all right and that the possibility of a tornado actually coming through the school was remote. On the other hand I also knew that bizarre things do happen and this could be the time for them.

Finally my classes were over for the day. I was in a horrible dilemma. Should I take out over the small country road and head for Raleigh or should I stay put until it was all over one way or another. I called home to the babysitter to see what the weather news was there. She said that so far nothing had been said at all about a tornado, just thunderstorms. So I decided to start out. It had been a hairy day and I was ready to call it quits and sit in my own living room for a while. The minute I hung up the phone my babysitter went back to the television set and there was not just tornado watches, but warnings. To the north of us one had just struck and one small one had been sighted around Raleigh. Before it was over we would have three to touch down in the Raleigh area. And this, of course, was where I was innocently headed!

When I started out there was a distinct yellow cast to the sky and very high winds; yet, it was reasonably clear. I assumed that since there were no warnings in Raleigh I was heading out of the disturbance area when in fact I was heading into it. About halfway home I noticed that the cloud cover was getting lower and darker and the wind was picking up. By then I was getting news from the Raleigh area on my car radio. I got so frightened that I stopped to get some advice from the farmers in a country store on the road. They advised me to keep going because I was just fourteen miles from real cover, a large church and a shopping center near it. I got back in my car figuring that if I drove about eighty I could be there in ten minutes. After about four more miles I looked across the low flat fields and realized that I was right in the path of a terrible storm, if not a tornado. I'd have to find some shelter, some place to stop. I knew that a large house was around the next curve in the road; I'd seen it on my trips back and forth for two years. I decided that I'd stop there, go up to the door, and beg for entrance. When I pulled into the driveway there were two cars in the back and I just knew someone was there. I ran to the front door and knocked. No answer. I knocked and rang until the wind really had picked up to an alarming strength and then the hail started slinging through the air the size of grade A medium eggs. I ran around to the back and got under a garage roof. Then the lightning started and I knew I had to get inside the house where I'd be safer. There was no way to explain to anyone later the panic that drove me actually to open the door of that house and walk in and stay there until the storm subsided. I can only say that I stood right at the back door ready to keep someone from shooting me if they were in the house, but asleep, or if someone drove up. The possibility of the latter was remote at this time since the roof of the porch next door flew by and two trees in the backyard of the house I was in slowly uprooted and fell in slow motion. All during this time I kept calling out, "Is anybody here?" Nobody ever answered and the house had that feel about it of being empty.

It appeared finally that the storm was slowing down. However, I wanted to be sure before I left my haven. I ran out to my car in the pouring rain and turned on my radio. It was then that the bulletins were coming fast and furious about the tornados touching down in Raleigh. Would I be running into them if I headed that way. Knowing that our area was not used to these storms I wondered if the reports were still accurate. I went back into the house and saw a telephone hanging on the wall. I picked it up and found that it was not long distance to Raleigh. So I called the best information I could get, my lawyer husband.

His professional and personal horror over my situation was divided between a breaking and entering charge and someone coming home and shooting me. He was not at all concerned over the storm, all dry and un-windblown in his fifth floor office in an exceptionally stable bank building. He assured me the storm was over in Raleigh and to get the hell out of there. I hung up miffed and misunderstood, and after all that horrible day I'd had.

He wouldn't know until later what a storm it had really been. In any case I realized that I was beginning to hear cars on the road again, so I went out, said goodbye to my friendly shelter and left.

Of course I got home all right and by the time I went back to the school the next week it was all a memory in my mind and in the kids' minds. They all wanted to know about my trip home and I told them most of it, but not all. I didn't want to set forth any bad examples. They were back to normal, cutting up, forgetting the day when we had sat in a huddle on the floor. I wondered how many of them would remember it in years to come and how many of them would someday write about the feelings of that day.

And then I thought how much like poetry all of this was and how much like teaching poetry. You can prepare for it and talk about it and learn all there is to know and when it's over you can describe it and discuss it and take it apart, but the soul of it and the center of it is done alone, feeling your own feelings, your own pulse, translating it from the foundation of your own experience. I can't do that for my students and don't try. I can only wish for them their own experiencing, their own souls, and their own ways of putting the world together.

III

BIBLIOGRAPHY

BIBLIOGRAPHY

The following collection of books rests on my shelves what time they're not in use. It is a collection which represents my personal interests: poetry, teaching, education, and children's books. Needless to say, not all of my books are listed here, just those I have found to be useful in the teaching of poetry or in other work in the schools. I have not listed any "little magazines" and not many single collections of poetry. I feel that they are too much a matter of taste to be of use to those interested in this book. For that same reason, I have listed only a few of the books I like on education, just those I really found helpful in the Poetry-in-the-Schools program.

I have listed some textbooks and some workbooks. The reason for this is that often we're in schools where teachers want to know if we know the names of some useful texts in the field of creative writing. Even though teaching poets only teach poetry, the teachers in the schools have to teach it all. Also I have found myself this year teaching a writing workshop which encompasses all phases of writing, which might happen to some of you sooner or later.

The anthologies, and indeed all of the books, are not meant to be an exhaustive or definitive list. They are all just books I've found or had given to me or heard about and ordered. Some may by now be in a difficult edition, or in paperback, or have new prices, so you may need to consult *Books in Print* to get updated information in some cases. So rummage through this list as you would a favorite bookstore and take what interests you. I offer this list not as an authority, but as a friend in the same field sharing my resources.

BOOKS ABOUT TEACHING POETRY

CHILDREN WRITE POETRY. By Flora Arnstein. Even though a bit dated, this is still a book to read. It is Ms. Arnstein's approach for a whole year of working with the same children. I feel her warm nature and good sense with the children and that in itself is something worth trying to learn. Dover, 1967. 216 pp. $2.00 (paperback).

LET THEM WRITE POETRY. By Nina Willis Walter (Out of Print). Although this author is a bit taken with some things I'm not, I still find parts of this book helpful. Considering what was going on when this book was written Ms. Walter was way ahead in her thinking. Holt, Rinehart and Winston, 1962. 179 pp. (paperback).

MATH, WRITING & GAMES IN THE OPEN CLASSROOM. By Herbert Kohl. Good suggestions, practical techniques for teaching writing to children from a man whom everyone in innovative education admires. The math part is a bonus. New York Review Book, 1974. $6.95 (hardbound). Random House. $2.45 (paperback).

POETRY 2—A Scholastic Literary Unit—Series 4100. Designed and edited by Stephen Dunning, M. Joe Eaton, and Malcolm Glass. This is the best unit available for classroom teachers for large classroom activity. They also have a POETRY 1 unit designed for the younger student. Any Scholastic representative will be happy to order sample units for you to look through. WORKBOOK, $1.95. TEACHING GUIDE, $6.95. POETRY USA, $.95. GRAB ME A BUS, $.75. SEARCH THE SILENCE, $.75. MAD, SAD, & GLAD. $.60.

ROSE, WHERE DID YOU GET THAT RED. By Kenneth Koch. A book formulated around teaching "great" poetry with the kids using the central "poetry idea" to write their own poems. Random House, 1973. $7.95 (hardbound). $2.45 (paperback).

WHAT'S INSIDE YOU IT SHINES OUT OF YOU. By Marc Kaminsky. An account of a young poet working with a group of older people in poetry. Has examples of their work. Horizon Press, 1974. $7.95 (hardbound).

THE WHOLE WORD CATALOGUE. Edited by Rosellen Brown, Marvin Hoffman, Martin Kushner, Phillip Lopate, and Sheila Murphy. Once the *only* word, now still the *best* word. A practical collection of ideas about writing designed for elementary and secondary students. Annotated bibliography. Teachers & Writers Collaborative, 1972. 72 pp. $4.00 (paperback).

THE WHOLE WORD CATALOGUE 2. Edited by Ron Padgett and Bill Zavatsky. The grand new handbook which contains a completely new collection of writing and art ideas for the elementary, secondary, and college classroom. Absolutely invaluable. Teachers & Writers Collaborative. 1976. 350 pp. $6.95 (paperback).

WISHES, LIES & DREAMS. By Kenneth Koch. A classic in its time. No poet should teach in a classroom without reading it and attaching his own values where they fit. Chelsea House, 1970. $7.95 (hardbound). Random House. $2.45 (paperback).

WORD MAGIC. By Charleen Whisnant and Jo Hassett. A good book by two North Carolina people, a poet and a teacher collaboration. Lots of ideas and practical advice from both views, inside the classroom with Jo Hassett and coming from the outside with Charleen Whisnant. Doubleday, 1974. 166 pp. $6.95 (hardbound).

BOOKS ON TEACHING CREATIVE WRITING OR WRITING WORKSHOPS OR ENGLISH COMPOSITION

BEING WITH CHILDREN. By Phillip Lopate. This is a comprehensive, witty and honest narrative account of a year spent in a city school in New York teaching kids in the fields of writing, theater, and videotape. It is a glorious reading treat full of good ideas, love, frustration, and courage. I can't imagine anyone not learning a lot from living in these pages. Doubleday, 1975. 392 pp. $7.95 (hardbound). Bantam, 1976. $1.95 (paperback).

CRAFT SO HARD TO LEARN: CONVERSATIONS WITH POETS AND NOVELISTS ABOUT THE TEACHING OF WRITING. Conducted by John Graham. Edited by George Garrett. A book which comes from taped interviews with John Graham of the University of Virginia for his radio program, "The Scholar's Bookshelf." Some of the contributors are R. V. Cassill, James Dickey, and Sylvia Wilkinson. Morrow Paperbacks, 1972. 93 pp. $1.45 (paperback).

CREATIVE CHOICES: A SPECTRUM OF QUALITY AND TECHNIQUE IN FICTION. By David Madden. A really different kind of teaching book and much needed. It is designed to acquaint the student with different styles and goes about it by reprinting short fiction from such different places as *Young Love, South Dakota Review, Galaxy,* and *Argosy.* A splendid idea, and great fun. Teacher's Guide. $.80. Scott, Foresman & Co., 1975. 245 pp. $5.00 (paperback).

A DAY DREAM I HAD AT NIGHT. By Roger Landrum. A collection of oral literature from children who were not learning to read well or write competently. Roger Landrum made class readers out of the children's own work, recorded the readers in a tape library, and designed a set of language exercises based on the readers. Teachers & Writers Collaborative, 1974 (Second Printing). 119 pp. $3.00 (paperback).

FIVE TALES OF ADVENTURE. By students at P.S. 75 in Manhattan. These stories cover a wide range of styles and interests. Other students think they're wonderful. A good stimulus for writing classes and for individual young writers. Virgil Books (published by Teachers & Writers Collaborative), 1975. 119 pp. $3.00, 10 copies or more at $2.00 (paperback).

IMAGINARY WORLDS. By Richard Murphy. A book about finding themes of sufficient breadth and interest to allow sustained independent writing by students. The way to do it and a body of student work are all here. Teachers & Writers Collaborative, 1974 (Second Printing), 111 pp. $3.00 (paperback).

IT'S MINE AND I'LL WRITE IT THAT WAY. By Dick Friedrich and David Kuester. I wish I had written this book, but just reading it will almost do. Two of the coolest guys around did write it using their own nutty-sane way of looking at the world, teaching writing, and themselves. For teaching attitudes and readability this book can't be beat. Random House (The College Dept.), 1972. 238 pp. $4.95 (paperback).

MAKE YOUR OWN COMICS FOR FUN AND PROFIT. By Richard Cummings. This is a perfect companion to TWC's newsletter issue (Vol. 8, Issue 1) on comic strips done by kids. It's an informally written how-to book using illustrations mostly by students. The four or five professional artists discussed are introduced by examples of work they did in their own school days. Plenty of good tips. Includes a valuable list of books for supplementary reading. Henry Z. Walck, Inc., 1976. 118 pp. $8.95 (hardbound).

ON CREATIVE WRITING. Edited by Paul Engle. A helpful collection of articles by specialists in the various creative writing disciplines. There are illustrative examples in each chapter. Dutton Paperback, 1966. 244 pp. $1.95.

PENCIL TO PRESS. By Marjorie Spector. This is a book about itself, about how it all came to be. The style is informal and highly informative. Most kids will ask sooner or later, "How do they make books?," or "How can I get a book published?" This book is a good answer. Good glossary. Lothrop, Lee and Shepard, 1975. 95 pp. $5.50 (hardbound).

SOMEBODY TURNED ON A TAP IN THESE KIDS. Edited by Nancy Larrick. This is mainly a collection of talks, papers read, and discussions coming out of the Poetry Festival sponsored by the School of Education of LeHigh University in 1969. It's a book alive with vision and humanity and one which I still consult repeatedly. Delacorte Press, 1971. $5.95 (hardbound). Dell, 1972. $2.45 (paperback).

SOMEONE LIKE ME. By Sheena Gillespie and Linda Stanley. This textbook is organized into interesting writing ideas with essays, stories, and poems following each one for clarity of idea. The organization and examples are first rate for composition classes. Winthrop Publishers, 1973. 332 pp. $4.95 (paperback).

TEACHING AND WRITING POPULAR FICTION: HORROR, ADVENTURE, MYSTERY AND ROMANCE IN THE AMERICAN CLASSROOM. By Karen M. Hubert. This is the only book I know of that explains how to teach students to write in popular genres. Every classroom should have a copy. Teachers will be intrigued and overjoyed with it and the kids will be hooked on trying to write stories with different slants. An invaluable and contemporary text. Virgil Books (published by Teachers & Writers Collaborative), 1976, 235 pp. $4.00 (paperback).

TURN NOT PALE, BELOVED SNAIL. By Jacqueline Jackson. This is called by the author, "a book about writing among other things." That is truly such an apt description that I hardly know what classification to place it under. The book is actually addressed to the young writer, but parents and teachers will love it too. Ms. Jackson obviously understands young people as well as the child in her own self, for she is never condescending, but always warm and sharing. Little, Brown and Company, 1974. 235 pp. $7.50 (hardbound).

WRITE. By Clement Stacy. For students in grades nine through twelve this collection presents writing samples, photographs and drawings, and starting points for specific writing assignments. All writing, photographs, etc. are pulled from the excellent TYPOG, a now defunct magazine which used to be a showplace for student writing. One of the best new "assignment type" books. Scott, Foresman & Co., 1974. 256 pp. $4.00.

WRITERS AS TEACHERS/TEACHERS AS WRITERS. Edited by Jonathan Baumbach. An excellent book. Teachers of writing who are writers themselves explore their methods and thoughts honestly. The reader gains from them, even if he's teaching first grade and they're talking about college students. I think the sections by Jonathan Baumbach and Wendell Berry are exceptional even in this quality collection. Holt, Rinehart and Winston, 1970. $5.95 (hardbound). $2.45 (paperback).

THE WRITER'S SENSE OF PLACE (South Dakota Review: Autumn 1975, Vol. 13, No. 3). Editor: John R. Milton. This is a collection of comments and essays solicited from fiction writers and poets across the country. The result is fascinating reading. Some of the poets represented are Gary Snyder, W. D. Snodgrass, Richard Hugo, Glenna Luschei, Karen Swenson, and William Stafford. South Dakota Review, Box 11, University Exchange, Vermillion, S. D. 57069. 1975. 139 pp. $2.50.

A WRITER TEACHES WRITING. By Donald Murray. This is halfway between being a book that teaches composition and one that teaches writing. I suppose you might say it's a creative way of teaching the former. In the back are hundreds of listings under "The Writing Teacher's Library," the best compilation I've ever seen and the most valuable. Houghton Mifflin, 1968. 256 pp. $6.95 (paperback).

WRITER TO WRITER. Edited by Floyd Watkins and Karl Knight. This is a series of readings on the craft of writing. It is divided into clear sections with contributors such as Thomas Wolfe, William Faulkner, Ernest Hemingway, and George Orwell. Totally absorbing. Houghton Mifflin, 1966. 243 pp. $5.25 (paperback).

THE YOUNG WRITEk AT WORK. By Jessie Rehder. Probably the best textbook ever written for the high school or college short fiction writing class. Here was a teacher who had both current

150

insight and spectacular vision. Bobbs-Merrill Co., 1962 (Sixth Printing, 1975). 274 pp. $4.75 (hardbound).

BOOKS ABOUT POETRY-IN-THE-SCHOOLS PROGRAMS

A BORROWER BE. Edited by Ruby Lee Norriss and Sally Harris Sange. Artists, dancers, photographers, poets all come together under the auspices of the Richmond Humanities Center to carry out "an interchange of culture in the classroom." The book about it is not only full of ideas, but is wonderfully inspiring. Richmond Humanities Center, One West Main Street, Richmond, Va. 23220. 1975. 89 pp. $2.00 (paperback).

A FEEL FOR WORDS. By Richard Fricks. An attractive book, easy to follow, with no really new ideas, but fresh approaches. Has a very interesting bibliography. Tennessee Arts Commission, 222 Capital Hill Building, Nashville, Tenn. 37219. 199 pp. $3.50 (paperback).

HOMEMADE POEMS. By Daniel Lusk. Lusk uses a delightful "anybody can play" approach to poetry in this lively, entertaining book. Many good ideas and examples. Format and information level excellent. Lame Johnny Press, 1974. Hermosa, S. D. 59 pp. $2.50 (paperback).

I AM AN UNKNOWN GREATNESS. Edited by David Long. A really beautiful anthology from Montana's 1974-75 Poetry-in-the-Schools Program. Has statements by the poets in the program. The poems used have an unusual strength and quality. The most important part to me is that the suggestions of method are always followed by good examples. Montana Arts Council, 235 East Pine, Missoula, Montana, 59801. 60 pp. $2.00 (paperback).

I WRITE WHAT I WANT: POETRY IN THE SCHOOLS. A wonderful hodge-podge of articles about, ideas for, and examples of the program in California. Lots of pictures, layout and cover make this an attractive book as well as helpful. San Francisco State Univ., San Francisco, Ca. 94132. 1975. 79 pp. $2.50 (paperback).

MY SISTER LOOKS LIKE A PEAR. By Douglas Anderson. A collection of good teaching ideas, some of the results, and an informal narrative account of his work in the schools by a poet teacher who's taught in ten Western and Midwestern States. Hart Publishing Company, 1974. 268 pp. $7.50 (hardbound).

THE NORTH WIND. From the Vermont Writers-in-the-Schools Program. This is a good anthology with each section headed up by a discussion of methods by the writers in the program. A lot of book for the money. Vermont Council on the Arts, 136 State Street, Montpelier, Vermont 05602. 82 pp. $.25 (paperback).

POEMMAKING: POETS IN CLASSROOMS. Edited by Ruth Whitman and Harriet Feinberg. A series of essays on teaching in the Poetry-in-the-Schools program by poet teachers in Massachusetts. Interesting to read and valuable to use in the classrooms. Massachusetts Council of Teachers of English, 205 Hampshire Street, Lawrence, Mass. 01841. 1975. 116 pp. $3.50 (paperback).

POETS IN THE SCHOOLS — 1972-73, 152 pp.
ARTISTS IN THE CLASSROOM — 1973, 143 pp.
Published by Connecticut Commission on the Arts: Poetry Programs. Connecticut has documented its programs in a more honest and informative way than any other area. The material to be ingested from these two books is important and timely. Conn. Commission on the Arts, 340 Capitol Ave., Hartford, Conn. 06106. Both of these are available free upon requests from individuals.

POETS IN THE SCHOOLS: A HANDBOOK. By Michael True. A short summary of what classroom teachers want to know about Poetry-in-the-Schools, National Council of Teachers of English, 1111 Kenyon Road, Urbana, Ill. 61801. 1976. 13 pp. $1.00 (paperback).

A ROAD NOT TAKEN. By David Verble (Published for the Tenn. Arts Commission and the "Poets-in-the-Schools" Program, Nashville, Tenn., 1973). This book offers a new approach to teaching poetry. Incorporates learning about poetry as well as how to write poetry. Has interesting ideas. Tenn. Arts Commission, 222 Capitol Hill Bldg., Nashville, Tenn. 37219. 92 pp. $2.00 (paperback).

THE TURTLIE AND THE TEACHER. Edited by Ruby Lee Norriss. Billed as "a dialogue between poets and students," it is much more. Poetry-in-the-Schools in Richmond was lucky to have Michael Mott, Dabney Stuart, and Sylvia Wilkinson there and we are lucky that they chose to document the visits. Philosophy and poetry and kids all kick around together to make a good book. Richmond Humanities Center, One West Main Street, Richmond, Va. 23220. 1974. 88 pp. $2.00 (paperback).

WESTERN STATES ARTS FOUNDATION STUDY. This group has just completed a study of the poetry and visual arts components of the Artists-in-the-Schools Program. This study has documented the effect of the program on artists, poets, school administrators, students, and teachers in ten states. The study is very impressive in its scope, information gathering techniques, and results. Available from the Arts Councils in all fifty states are the Study Highlights, Study Summary, Technical Report, and a film. Please be sure to contact the agency in your state and not the Foundation itself. For additional information, however, you may write them at 1517 Market, Denver, Colorado, 80202.

There are many fine anthologies of student work coming out of the Poetry-in-the-Schools program in every State. Inquiries about them can be sent to the States' Arts Council. For listings see back of A DIRECTORY OF AMERICAN POETS (see address in this bibliography) or send $2.00 to the Associated Councils of the Arts, Room 820, 1564 Broadway, New York, N. Y. 10036, and they will send you a list.

PLACES THAT ACCEPT AND PUBLISH THE WORK OF STUDENTS

HANGING LOOSE. Edited by Robert Hershon, Emmett Jarrett, Dick Lourie, Ron Schrieber. Roughly 10 pages an issue devoted to work by high school students. Need to enclose a note with brief biography and please only send 6-7 poems. Will soon publish an anthology drawn from their high school section with comments by the poets. A forerunner in this area. They just published a book by one of their early high school poets. 231 Wyckoff St., Brooklyn, N. Y. 11217. 4 issues, $5.50. Sample, $1.50.

SEVENTEEN. Publishes poems, first-person articles, and short pieces by teenagers in every issue. Have an annual short story contest. Like work sent by individuals, not class project submissions. You can write them for rules on submissions and they'll send those in addition to lots of other helpful information. 320 Park Ave., New York, N. Y. 10022.

SCOPE: For junior high, low ability, low interest students.
VOICE: Higher ability, average students in both junior and senior high.
LITERARY CALVACADE: For academically gifted students in both junior and senior high.

These magazines all give opportunity for student submissions from time to time. They also run annual contests. If your school doesn't get them automatically, individuals can subscribe. Scholastic Magazines Service, 50 W. 44th St., New York, N.Y. 10036. Published monthly during school year.

STONE SOUP. Edited by William Rubel and Gerry Mandel. Has stories, poems, plays, book reviews and drawings by children ages 4-12. Children need to send a self-addressed stamped envelope to get stuff back and everything should be labeled with name and age. This is a superior publication. Editors Notebook-Guide for Teachers, $1.75 for 1 year (3 issues). Box 83, Santa Cruz, Ca. 95063. One year, $5.00. One copy, $2.00. Published three times a year.

In addition to the above:

Many states have English journals which sponsor contests for students or take student work for a special issue.

Also there are youth publications in every church which publish student work of all kinds, not just that which is religious in nature.

BOOKS ABOUT POETRY

AN INTRODUCTION TO HAIKU. Translations and Commentary by Harold Henderson. The definitive work on haiku. Doubleday Anchor Book, 1958. 190 pp. $1.95 (paperback).

AN INTRODUCTION TO POETRY. By X. J. Kennedy. Very good. A leader among books of this type. Strong poems and good statements. Teacher manual free. Little, Brown, and Co., 1974. $5.95 (paperback).

HOW DOES A POEM MEAN. By John Ciardi. The major text on poetry by the "old pro." This book still outclasses everything else for use in senior high and college classes. Adults also find it monumentally educational. Houghton Mifflin Co., 1959. $5.95 (paperback). 2nd Edition, Ciardi & Miller Williams, 1975. $5.50 (paperback).

HOW TO REVISE YOUR OWN POEMS. By Anne Hamilton (Out of Print). Even though this book is out of print, it's one to try to find in a library or elsewhere. Has good tips. The Writer, Inc.

THE POETICS OF THE NEW AMERICAN POETRY. Edited by Donald Allen and Warren Tallman. A series of essays by such policy making poets as Ezra Pound, Hart Crane, W. C. Williams, Robert Creeley and Charles Olson. Widely known statements together in one volume. Evergreen Press, 1973. 463 pp. $3.95 (paperback).

POETRY AS DISCIPLINED PLAY. By Robert Francis (Out of Print). A good book to take a look at if you can find it. Scott Foresman, 1967.

POETRY IS. By Ted Hughes. This is meant to be an introduction to the world of poetry for young readers, based on Hughes' B.B.C children's programs. I use it as an approach to teaching older kids to write, grouping poems around certain subject areas as examples. A valuable book. Doubleday, 1967. 101 pp. $1.95 (paperback).

SOUND & SENSE. By Laurence Perrine. A textbook which is meant as an introduction to poetry. Even though a college text, it has a lot to offer to anybody. It's a staple in most schools. Instructors manual available. Harcourt Brace Jovanovich, 1973 (4th Ed.). 732 pp. $4.95 (paperback).

MAGAZINES AND NEWSLETTERS

AMERICAN POETRY REVIEW. Edited by Stephen Berg, Rhoda Schwartz, David Bonanno and Arthur Vogelsang. One of the leading publications on poetry today. Comes in newspaper format, imparts gossip as well as the gospel. Every poet I know subscribes to it. Also has special Poetry-in-the-Schools section every issue that's excellent. Dept. A, Temple University Center City, 1616 Walnut St., Room 405, Philadelphia, Pa. 19103. One year, $5.00. Published six times a year.

LEARNING: THE MAGAZINE FOR CREATIVE TEACHING. Editor: Morton Malkofsky. Not every issue carries creative writing ideas, but the November, 1976, issue was a language arts special which was very helpful and informative. *Learning,* 530 University Avenue, Palo Alto, Ca. 94301. 1976. 108 pp. $1.50 (for November issue).

POETRY NOW. Edited by E. V. Griffith. Another newspaper format. Magazine always leads with an interview, then reviews current poetry books by printing poems from them. A good way to do things, and most exciting and informative. 3118 K St., Eureka, Ca. 95501. One year, $5.00. One copy, $1.25. Published six times a year.

SPARROW PAMPHLET SERIES. Appears monthly. Prints poetry, fiction, essays, criticisms. Each issue is the work of single author. Good material for classroom. Black Sparrow Press, Box 25603, Los Angeles, Ca. 90025. $.50.

THE TEACHERS & WRITERS MAGAZINE. Draws together the experience and ideas of the writers and other artists who conduct T & W workshops in schools and community groups. Detailed work diaries, works of students, along with outside contributors. A magazine out front. Try to get as many back issues as available. 186 W. 4th St., New York, N. Y. 10014. One year, $5.00. One issue, $2.00. Published three times yearly.

TRELLIS. Edited by Margaret Anderson, Winston Fuller and Irene McKinney. The first issue and supplement of this new magazine are tremendously exciting. There are articles and poems and all sorts of stuff thrown in. In the supplement, the readership gets to "answer" anything they want to that was in the previous issue. Lots of material for the teaching poet to plug into. Box 656, Morgantown, W. V. 26505. Publish one issue and one supplement a year. Two issues and two supplements, $12.00.

WEST COAST POETRY REVIEW. Edited by William Fox. An issue devoted to the Poetry-in-the-Schools Program is still available. 1127 Codel Way, Reno, Nevada 89503. Summer, 1973 issue. $1.50.

POETRY ANTHOLOGIES OR BOOKS

ANTHOLOGY OF CONCRETE POETRY. Edited by Emmett Williams. Something Else Press, 1967. $3.95 (paperback).

ARROW BOOK OF FUNNY POEMS. Collected by Eleanor Clymer. Even though this book is a bit old the collection of humor poems in it is still top notch. Scholastic Press, 1961. 96 pp. $.25 (paperback).

THE BAT POET. By Randall Jarrell. Illustrated by Maurice Sendak. There is no way that children (or adults) who write can help but associate themselves with the brown bat who stayed awake days to see the world in a new way. As bat poet he tries to make the other bats see as he does. A charming fable. Good poems throughout. Macmillan Co., 1967 (Sixth Printing). 43 pp. $3.95 (hardbound).

THE BLACK POETS. Edited by Dudley Randall. An excellent anthology from a few years back which starts with a section on "Folk Poetry" and moves to poetry of the 1960's. Emphasis on contemporary poets. Bantam, 1971. 353 pp. $1.65 (paperback).

A BOOK OF ANIMAL POEMS. Selected by William Cole. Illustrated by Robert Andrew Parker. An absolutely marvelous collection of poems marked by a large variety of animals and poets. Wonderfully lacking in the choices is any poem verging on sentimentality. Viking Press, 1973. 288 pp. $8.95 (hardbound).

THE BOOK OF IMAGINARY BEINGS. By Jorge Luis Borges with Margarita Guerrero. Revised, enlarged, and translated by Norman Thomas di Giovanni. Not poetry, but short discussions of strange beings from the reasonably common Minotaur to the uncommon, homely, and mournful Squonk of Pennsylvania which thwarts capture by dissolving itself in its own tears. Students like to write stories and poems about the creatures in the book and they like to make up their own. Avon Books, 1969. 265 pp. $1.45 (paperback).

THE CONTEMPORARY AMERICAN POETS. Edited by Mark Strand. Good overall coverage but only one to three poems per poet. Meridian, 1969. 390 pp. $3.95 (paperback).

CRICKET SONGS. Translated by Harry Behn. A wonderful collection of Japanese haiku illustrated with pictures selected from Japanese masters. Harcourt Brace Jovanovich, 1967. $2.50 (hardbound).

THE DOG WRITES ON THE WINDOW WITH HIS NOSE. Edited by David Kherdian. Illustrated by Nonny Hogrogian. A perfect selection of beginning contemporary poems for children ages five to eight. Kherdian believes that "the best poetry for children is poetry that is written for adults—but judiciously selected." This is a belief dear to my heart and so obviously full of merit that I'm surprised it isn't a way of life for publishers. However, Mr. Kherdian seems to be among the first to collect a quality anthology for readers so young. The pictures, by the way, are good enough to send chills of joy up and down the spine. Four Winds Press, 1977. 31 pp. $5.95 (hardback).

157

EGO-TRIPPING. By Nikki Giovanni. A picture book collection of poems about the experience of being Black. A very special significant book for children. Lawrence Hill & Co., 1973. 37 pp. $2.95 (paperback).

THE ENDURING BEAST. Edited and illustrated by Miriam Beerman. Don't be mislead by the gorgeous illustrations into thinking this is an elementary school book. The poems constitute an excellent animal collection but include tough poems like May Sevenson's "Feel Like a Bird" and Ned O'Gorman's "The Rhino Stands Still In a Field of Lilies." Doubleday & Co., 1972. 64 pp. $4.95 (hardbound).

A FIRST READER OF CONTEMPORARY AMERICAN POETRY. Edited by Patrick Gleeson. One of my favorite anthologies. It is what it says, "a first reader," an excellent introduction to poetry. The poets and styles are varied, but all poems have high interest level. Charles E. Merrill, 1969. 189 pp. $3.50 (paperback).

FIRST VOICES. (the first book, the second book, the third book, the fourth book). Edited by Geoffrey Summerfield. One of the best series of anthologies for students from seven to twelve. They were published at one time in the United States by Random House and I bought one of mine from a remainder table. The others I bought in England (called there *Junior Voices*), hence the strange information that follows. Penguin Educational Books, Harmondsworth, Middesex, England. 1970-1975. 60 pence (paperback).

HOSANNAH THE HOME RUN. Edited by Alice Fleming. Poems about sports, including the usual as well as unusual ones, with authors ranging from Virgil to Gregory Corso. A book to entice those junior high sports enthusiasts to poetry. Little, Brown and Co., 1972. 68 pp. $4.95 (hardbound).

IT IS THE POEM SINGING INTO YOUR EYES. Edited by Arnold Adoff. This is an anthology I love and my students love. There is great variety here and great appeal. It was the anthology which first showed me just how well young people relate to each other's work. Harper & Row, 1972. 128 pp. $1.95 (paperback).

I, TOO, SING AMERICA: BLACK VOICES IN AMERICAN LITERATURE. By Barbara Stanford. Poetry, short story, non-fiction, book excerpts. One of the first "Black Studies" texts to come my way a number of years ago. It holds up well. Hayden, 1971. 308 pp.

THE ME NOBODY KNOWS. Edited by S. M. Joseph. The first collection of prose and poetry written by ghetto children to have nationwide impact. Avon, 1969. 144 pp. $.95 (paperback).

MESSAGES. Edited by X.J. Kennedy. This is an anthology arranged by themes, which is most helpful if you like to teach that way. I like the variety of poets represented and the numerous styles. In the section devoted to poems about solitude W.S. Merwin might have a poem right next to one by Wordsworth. You don't know it without looking in the back, since there are no names on the poems to influence the reader. An excellent section in the back combines bibliography and biographical information. Also has a glossary of terms. Little, Brown and Company, 1973.

MINDSCAPES: POEMS FOR THE REAL WORLD. Edited by Richard Peck. An excellent anthology for the junior and senior high student. A good place to gather examples from when you're teaching certain poetry ideas. Delacorte Press, 1971. 165 pp. $4.95 (hardbound).

NAKED POETRY. Edited by Stephen Berg and Robert Mezy. A study of "recent American poetry in open forms." Presents large sections of poems by one poet, then a statement by that poet. This is still one of the best books around. Bobbs-Merrill, 1969. 387 pp. $2.95 (paperback).

PICK ME UP. Edited by William Cole. A book of short short poems from all sources and from the old masters to contemporary poets. High quality, high interest level, for all ages, but especially for the young. A handy book for a teacher to keep on her desk. Macmillan Co., 1972. 183 pp. $4.95 (hardbound).

POEMS CHILDREN WILL SIT STILL FOR: A SELECTION FOR THE PRIMARY GRADES. Edited by Beatrice de Regniers, Eva Moore and Mary Michaels White. I like this anthology if it's used in connection with others. All the poems rhyme, but the choices of poems are good and include many for primary grades not usually found in their books. One really good feature is a biographical index that contains a short paragraph about each poet which includes things a child would understand and care about. Citation Press, 1969. 128 pp. $1.85 (paperback).

POETRY HERE AND NOW. Edited by David Kherdian. Linoleum cuts by Nonny Hogrogian. Another good anthology for the young student, but this time perhaps between ten and twelve. These poems are a bit longer than the others in Mr. Kherdian's book mentioned earlier and a bit more complex from an emotional sense, but they still hold interest, are lively, and contemporary. Back has short biographies of the poets included. Greenwillow Books, 1976, 64 pp. $5.95 (hardback).

THE POETRY OF BLACK AMERICA: ANTHOLOGY OF THE 20TH CENTURY. Edited by Arnold Adolf. Undoubtedly the best anthology of Black poetry I've read. Adolf uses many poets who are not widely known now but who will be eventually. Also I really like his choices of poems. He is in touch with what is happening and he has a fine ear. Harper & Row, 1973. 552 pp. $12.50 (hardbound).

THE POETRY OF THE NEGRO: 1746-1970. Edited by Langston Hughes and Arna Bontemps. A definitive collection, more traditional in approach than the Randall book. Doubleday Anchor Book, 1970 (New Edition). 645 pp. $4.95 (paperback).

PRAYERS FROM THE ARK. By Carmen Bernes de Gasztold. These simple poem-prayers by different creatures appeal to children. They have the extra virtue of being in free verse. Viking Compass Book, 1969. 71 pp. $1.25 (paperback).

REFLECTIONS ON A GIFT OF WATERMELON PICKLE. Edited by Stephen Dunning, Edward Lueders, Hugh Smith. A good anthology to use in elementary schools and middle schools. I wish there weren't so many rhyming poems, but I've still used my copy until it's ragged. Comes as part of a Scholastic unit, but can be bought in hardcover in bookstores. Lothrop, Lee, & Shepard Co., 1966. 139 pp. $4.50 (hardbound).

SEASON SONGS. By Ted Hughes. Pictures by Leonard Baskin. A very sophisticated book, and beautiful. Hughes addresses the subject of seasons with plain words in elegant combinations. These poems help the older student understand how to write about nature without gushing cliches. Viking Press, 1975. 77 pp. $10.00 (hardbound).

SELECTED TRANSLATIONS, 1948-1968. By W. S. Merwin. An excellent, interesting range of work including translations from the Eskimo, Chinese, Irish, Greek, Latin, French, Spanish, and

Russian. Antheneum. 176 pp. $2.95 (paperback).

SHAKING THE PUMPKIN: TRADITIONAL POETRY OF THE INDIAN NORTH AMERICAS. Edited by Jerome Rothenberg. A valuable book for studying and appreciating tradition, rhythms, and mystery. Many poets-in-schools use it in different ways. Doubleday Anchor Book, 1972. 476 pp. $3.95 (paperback).

SOME HAYSTACKS DON'T EVEN HAVE ANY NEEDLE. Edited by Stephen Dunning, Edward Lueders, Hugh Smith. I use this all the time in junior and senior high schools. An excellent collection for anybody, but especially pertinent to the young adult reader. Modern art which accompanies poems is real bonus. Scott, Foresman, & Co., 1969. 191 pp. $5.95 (hardbound).

SPORTS POEMS. Edited by R. R. Knudson and P. K. Ebert. A book widely used by poets working in schools. Dell, 1971. $.75 (paperback).

VISUAL LANGUAGE. By Richard Kostelanetz. Concrete poetry by a leader in the genre. Assembling Press, 1970. $2.00 (paperback).

VOICES OF THE RAINBOW: CONTEMPORARY POETRY BY AMERICAN INDIANS. Edited by Kenneth Rosen. There is much to be gained by the young poet in studying the Indian "voice." The traditions and mythology of the past obviously affect these poets, yet they definitely interpret them in a new light. The organic integration of the symbolic aspects of nature and concrete objects seen in most of the poems by the American Indian is a lesson yet unlearned by many poets. The Viking Press, 1975. 232 pp. $10.00.

WE BECOME NEW: POEMS BY CONTEMPORARY AMERICAN WOMEN. Edited by Lucille Iverson and Kathryn Ruby. My favorite anthology by women poets. Full and interesting representation by the best poets writing today. Bantam, 1975. 234 pp. $2.25 (paperback).

WHERE THE SIDEWALK ENDS. By Shel Silverstein. Poems and drawings by one of the masters of humor. His use of his skills in the field of children's literature is a gift to everyone. This book is a smash hit. Harper and Row, 1974. 166 pp. $6.89 (hardbound).

THE WHISPERING WIND: POETRY BY YOUNG AMERICAN INDIANS. Edited by Terry Allen. Collection of poetry written by young poets at the Institute of American Indian Arts. Very self-explanatory. Interesting to other young people because of such true reflection of life style. Doubleday, 1972. 128 pp. $1.95 (paperback).

ZERO MAKES ME HUNGRY. Compiled by Edward Lueders and Primus St. John. Lueders is one of the three compilers of *Haystacks* and *Reflections* (see above). His new collaborator is a good poet and teacher who knows all about working in the schools. So, these poems make an excellent collection for the teaching poet as well as school libraries. The book is not as elegantly designed as the two mentioned above, but the poems are every bit as good. Lothrop, Lee & Shepard, 1976. 143 pp. $6.95.

EDUCATION RESOURCE BOOKS

BIG ROCK CANDY MOUNTAIN. (No longer being printed. Back copies available). Probably the biggest loss to experimental education in this country occurred when this magazine folded. It had the most interesting pages I've ever read, full of stuff so far removed from everything else that it soared. Try to get all back issues available. February, 1971 was an issue devoted to children's writing. 1115 Merril Street, Menlo Park, Ca. 94025.

THE COURAGE TO CREATE. By Rollo May. A slender book full of insight for those who create and/or those who are trying to get others to create. Bantam, 1975. 173 pp. $1.95 (paperback).

HOW TO SURVIVE IN YOUR NATIVE LAND. By James Herndon. I re-read this book from time to time to gain perspective in the schools. Mr. Herndon is a "grade A" teacher and a "triple A" human being. The combination makes reading about his teaching experiences always at very least, a pleasure. Simon & Schuster, 1971. $5.95 (hardbound). Bantam, 1972. $1.25 (paperback).

HUMANISTIC EDUCATION SOURCEBOOK. Edited by Donald Read and Sidney Simon. A sourcebook of articles combining in one volume the major contributions to the rapidly expanding and workable theory of humanistic education. Fantastic bibliography. Prentice-Hall, 1975. 482 pp. $14.17 (hardbound).

OPEN SESAME. By Evelyn Carswell and Darrell Roubinek. Although this is meant to be a primer on "openess in the educational environment," it is a valuable book for anyone who works with kids in any subject. Full of interesting excerpts and illustrations by top educators. Goodyear Publishing Company, Pacific Palisades, Ca. 90272. 1974. 287 pp. $4.95 (paperback).

RESOURCE AND REFERENCE BOOKS

CODA. Published six times a year by Poets and Writers. It is full of all manner of announcements, short articles, and helpful information. Published by Poets and Writers (see address below). $5.00 a year.

A DIRECTORY OF AMERICAN FICTION WRITERS: 1976 EDITION. Also published by Poets and Writers. An important reference work listing 800 contemporary fiction writers in this country. It also has the same good information for fiction writers as its poetry counterpart. (See address below.) 127 pp. $10.00 (hardbound). $5.00 (paperback).

A DIRECTORY OF AMERICAN POETS: 1975 EDITION. Published by Poets and Writers, Inc. This and the companion newsletter, *Coda*, constitute the most comprehensive, up-to-date, and therefore, valuable, unit for poets today. The *Directory* not only lists poets but also agencies and schools dealing with poetry in every state. In addition it has excellent listings of anthologies, films, videotapes, reference sources for creative writing teachers, literary organizations, and bookstores in every state which specialize in poetry. 201 W. 54th St., New York, N. Y. 10019. Published yearly. $12.00 (hardbound). $6.00 (Paperback).

THE ELEMENTS OF STYLE. By William Strunk, Jr. and E. B. White. There's no doubt in my mind (and most other people's) that this is still the best book on the fundamentals of writing. It is so elegantly written that I still periodically read it just for pleasure. Macmillan, 1972 (Second Edition). $3.50 (hardbound). $1.25 (paperback).

HARPER DICTIONARY OF CONTEMPORARY USAGE. By William and Mary Morris (with the assistance of a panel of 136 distinguished consultants on usage). If in doubt about the rapidly changing world of words, then this is a good source of information. The only problem is that one word in this book is like one potato chip. You can't get by with just one and you'll end up reading for a long time. Harper and Row, 1975. 650 pp. $15.00.

INTERNATIONAL DIRECTORY OF LITTLE MAGAZINES AND SMALL PRESSES. Edited by Len Fulton. Gives information to writers including the listings, editors, addresses, subscription prices and so on. Infinite details to help the writer decide almost everything about where to submit for publication. Published yearly by Dustbooks, Box 1056, Paradise, Ca. 95969. $9.95 (hardbound). $6.95 (paperback).

POETRY HANDBOOK: A DICTIONARY OF TERMS. By Babette Deutsch. Exactly what it says it is. An excellent reference book. Funk & Wagnalls, 1969 (Third Edition). 202 pp. $2.95 (paperback).

A PRACTICAL STYLE GUIDE FOR AUTHORS AND EDITORS. By Margaret Nicholson. Good, cheap, and easier to follow than the MLA STYLE SHEET. Holt, 1967. 143 pp. $1.75 (paperback).

QUESTIONS YOU ALWAYS WANTED TO ASK ABOUT ENGLISH (BUT WERE AFRAID TO RAISE YOUR HAND). By Maxwell Nurnberg. A funny and human guide to English usage. Memorable examples for junior and senior highs (mothers and fathers too!). Pocket Books, 1972. 258 pp. $1.25 (paperback).

REFERENCE DEPT. — THE LIBRARY OF CONGRESS. There are many speeches by poets printed up and sold which I find to be both interesting and timely. Even one from years ago helps give perspective to today's poetry world. For a list write to: Superintendent of Documents, U. S. Government Printing Office, Washington, D.C. 20402.

REVERSE DICTIONARY. By Theodore M. Bernstein. An unusual and wonderful reference book. Here you look up the meanings and they lead you to the very word you're looking for plus some you weren't. Quadrangle Press, 1975. 277 pp. $10.00.

WRITER'S MARKET. Edited by Jane Koester and Rose Adkins. Markets for everything worth writing (and some that aren't). Good information as usual from this leader in the field of information. Writer's Digest Press. Published yearly.

IV

APPENDIXES

APPENDIX A
Obligations of Schools and Evaluation Forms

Letter to schools notifying acceptance in program, name of poet, and date of visit.

October   1972

Dear

Your school is one of the sixty schools that has been chosen to participate in the Poetry-in-the-Schools Program in North Carolina this year. We were convinced last year that this was one of the best programs ever offered the young people in our State. Hopefully this year will be even better. Many schools requested this program that had to be turned down for lack of funds in our grant. Because of this if you feel at this time that you can not participate as previously expected please call this office immediately and resign from the program. Needless to say, in a program of this large range we will not be able to change the dates given you except in cases of dire necessity. Please request the faculty and principal of your school to schedule other major events during other weeks in order to insure good attention for the poet's week-in-residence.

Enclosed you will find (1) a resume of the obligations of the host school; (2) general information about the program; (3) information about your poet; (4) an invitation to the conference in Raleigh on November 3. Please read everything carefully and bring any questions you have with you to Raleigh. Keep all that we send you in a safe place. You will need it for reference in the weeks before your poet arrives and also the week he is there. Be sure to pay particular attention to the times when schedules, evaluations, and booklets are due in this office.

I hope the program will be as successful in your school as it has been in others. If there is anything I can do to help you in any way please call on me.

Best regards,

(Mrs.) Ardis Kimzey, Coordinator
Poetry in the Schools Program
Division of Cultural Arts
Telephone: 829-7467

Poet: PLEASE ACKNOWLEDGE THIS
Dates of Visit: MAILING

Conference Invitation

POETRY-IN-THE-SCHOOLS CONFERENCE

November 3—Friday—10 A.M.-5 P.M.

Community Hall South:
Crabtree Valley
Raleigh, N.C.

Crabtree Valley is the new shopping center just outside Raleigh on Highway 70 (Durham Highway). The Community Hall South is beside Thalheimer's on the lower level under the back parking deck.

We will meet in the Hall at 10 A.M. The morning session will be divided between a question and answer period and a panel discussion involving some of the poets in last year's program.

The break for lunch will be at 12:30 P.M. at which time everybody will be on his own. There are many fine restaurants on the mall.

It is suggested that school representatives and poets use some of this time to get acquainted and discuss schedules and other matters pertaining to their visits. Before we meet for the afternoon session, participants are also urged to browse through the materials displayed on the tables at the rear of the room.

The afternoon session will begin promptly at 2:30 P.M. and will be turned over to the poets for a poetry reading. This was the highlight of last year's meeting, so we moved it to the afternoon in order that the school representatives might attend.

The program will end at approximately 4:30 P.M. There will be a social hour immediately following in the same area for those who can stay. There will be a slight charge of $2.00 a person since we can't take funds from our program for this. Please fill out the enclosed form and mail it back as soon as possible.

The schools are encouraged to send as many students, teachers, and principals to the conference as they would like, even though only one representative is required. (Remember to add $2.00/person for the social hour.) The travel expenses of the school representatives must be taken care of by the individual school systems. The poets will be paid mileage and will be given forms for this purpose at the meeting. They are also invited to bring friends with them.

School Guidelines and General Information

OBLIGATIONS OF SCHOOLS: GENERAL OUTLINE

(All of these are explained in detail on the following pages)

1. Pay the poet $100 as part of the week's payment and expenses.

2. Send evaluations from each student, teacher, and administrator involved in this program to the State office.

3. Appoint a chairman for the project who is able to direct the program in each school and who will attend the conference in Raleigh on November 3.

4. Help the poet compile a booklet of student work.

5. Provide the poet with any audio-visual aid he or she requests.

6. Operate under the basic teaching plan.

1. **Finances**

The school should be prepared in advance to give the poet a check for $100 upon completion of the visit on Friday. This can be of major importance to those poets who plan to use the money to pay motel bills upon leaving the school.

2. **Evaluations**

Enclosed you will find two sample evaluation forms, one for teachers and administrators and one for students. Please reproduce these in any manner available to you. We must have an evaluation from each student, teacher, and administrator involved in your program. Please send two copies (they can be xeroxed or carbon copies) of each evaluation to the State Office within three weeks after the poet's visit.

3. **Program Chairman**

The program chairman works directly with the poet in setting up, carrying out, and completing the program in her school. She or he is responsible for everything that appears in the "obligations of the schools" outline.

4. **Samples of Student Work and Booklets**

It is required that we have a sample selection of student work for the National Endowment office. Our office also requires such a collection from which poems will be chosen to appear in the student anthology to be published at the completion of this year's program. (Copies of last year's anthology are available from Publications, Room 352, State Department of Public Instruction, Education Building, Raleigh, North Carolina, 27602, at $1.50 a copy.)

It is best for these samples to be put in a booklet, any kind you or the students might choose to make. There will be samples from last year on display at the conference. In many cases the students did the designs for the booklets and they were excellent. As chairman this booklet will be primarily your responsibility.

Following is one method suggested for compiling this work. Each day the poet takes home the work done that day, checks and edits (if necessary and/or desirable) the poems that he or she wants included in the booklet. Sometimes the poet will take home Friday's work and return it by mail to the school. After receiving all poems the poet has chosen, the chairman should check those poems against a class role of participating students. If any student is not represented, the chairman should select a poem by that student for the booklet. Also, the chairman and other teachers involved should include any poems written during the week that they would like to see considered for the anthology. Please see that the student's full name (first and last) is on each poem and also his grade level.

When the booklet is finished there should be enough copies made to pass to each student in the program as well as several for the school library. Send two copies of the booklet to this office and two copies to the poet. These should be in the mail no later than three weeks after the poet leaves.

5. Audio-Visual Aid

Most poets use record players, slide projectors, and movie projectors in their work. Check with your poet before he or she arrives to see what equipment he will require, and please have it in good working order. It is especially necessary to have a good record player as almost everybody uses music.

6. Schedules and Teaching Plans

a) Selection of students—In many schools students signed up for this program according to interest. This seemed to work well and made it possible for students on all levels to participate and not just those in the advanced classes. This is good, for the program is designed to reach all students, not just those with a particular intelligence level. Enthusiasm for the program or simply for a new learning experience should be the criteria for participation. The poets from last year have suggested that each class should not exceed thirty students and we would like chairpersons to honor this preference.

b) Teacher preparation—Before the poet arrives, get the group of teachers together who will be involved in the program and go over the materials mailed to you. Stress to them the importance of staying in the room while the poet is teaching. They, as well as the students, are supposed to gain from the visit. It is a good idea to have the teacher conference on Monday so that the teacher and poet can get acquainted at the very beginning of the visit.

c) Location—Because the poet will come carrying much equipment and many books it is necessary for him or her to be given one place to stay in and teach in for the duration of the week. This is also important since the poets like for the students to know where to locate them if they want to discuss poetry between classes or in free periods.

171

d) Basic teaching plan—The poets will spend four hours a day teaching four different groups of students either in class or workshops and will have one teacher seminar during school hours or after school. The basic plan used to include one reading, but some of the poets believed that large readings accomplished little so far as the program's goals were concerned. Many prefer to incorporate their own material into the program in the daily class periods. We decided to leave the question of readings up to the schools and the individual poets.

The following ideas were formulated as examples of how the four hours of teaching might be broken up: 1) four sections of students for five days at one hour per section; 2) two hours in the morning with about forty students and two hours in the afternoon with forty more each day for five days; 3) for the first three days have the poet teach four sections of students and use the last two days for open residency (the poet stays in one room and the students come to him or her when they can).

A lot of schools like to leave one of the four teaching periods open for the poet to have private conferences with students.

Remember that however the plan is divided it is not intended to reach masses of students, superficially, but to reach smaller groups in depth.

THE TEACHING PLANS ARE PURELY SUGGESTIONS AND SHOULD BE DISCUSSED AND WORKED OUT WITH YOUR POET. HE MAY HAVE ANOTHER IDEA ABOUT THE WAY HE WANTS TO WORK. IT IS OF UTMOST IMPORTANCE FOR THE TEACHING SCHEDULE TO BE COMFORTABLE FOR BOTH THE POET AND THE SCHOOL.

e) A copy of the schedule should be sent to the poet and to this office three weeks in advance of the poet's visit. This will give plenty of time for changes if they are necessary and will avoid last minute misunderstandings about the work plans.

GENERAL INFORMATION

Transportation

The poets are responsible for their transportation to the town in which your school is located. Some of them will come with other poets in the area and some may come by bus. Please clear this with your poet and find out in advance if they will need transportation while working in your school.

Meals

The poets have an expense account which includes meals. It is up to each individual teacher and poet as to whether they will extend and accept invitations to meals. Most of the poets who arrive in town on Sunday do appreciate being asked to dinner that night simply to get acclimated to the surroundings and to hear if there are any last minute changes in the schedule.

Lodging

The poets have housing provisions in their expense accounts. The poet may call on you to help locate a motel, boarding house, or private home that takes in guests. Please help him or her in this matter if you can and I'm sure the poet would be glad to have specific recommendations if you have any.

Publicity

There are two areas of publicity in which you will want to participate: in your school, and in your community. In the school it is a good idea to form a publicity committee comprised of students. Notices on the bulletin board, in the school paper, and in class letters are good. Enclosed you will find a picture of your poet to be used however you wish, but these must be returned to the state office. Last year one of the schools had a student draw a picture of their poet and it was put on an easel outside the library door. Also enclosed are some samples of the poet's work. It can be mimeographed and distributed to classes for discussion before the poet arrives. If the school publicity is left to the students they can find many ingenious ways to reach their friends.

Publicity in the community depends on how receptive local papers and radio and TV studios are. Most of them are anxious for any newsworthy event and will give lots of coverage if notified in time. There could be announcements of the poet's arrival and then a follow-up feature story with pictures in the local newspaper. (The picture mentioned earlier could be used in the paper before the poet arrives.) Radio and TV stations usually have some interview programs that would be delighted to have a writer on the show.

We would appreciate two copies of any newspaper coverage. Also, please remember to send the poet a copy.

POETRY-IN-THE-SCHOOLS

EVALUATION: TEACHER AND ADMINISTRATORS

What type student did the program reach in your school?

How do you feel the students in your school benefited from this experience?

Did you feel that your poet was effective with the students?

Do you think the week will have a continuing influence on your students?

How do you feel you can best insure this continuing interest?

What did you like best and least about the program?

Would you want this program in your school again?

Please include a schedule of the poet's week.

What was done in your school and community to give publicity to your poet's visit?

Name: _____

Title: _____.

School: _____

174

POETRY-IN-THE-SCHOOLS

EVALUATION: STUDENT
(The student does not have to sign this)

Has this program changed your attitudes about reading and writing poetry? How?

What did you like best and least about the program?

How would you set up the program in your school if you were doing it?

Do you think you could have been better prepared for your poet's visit? How?

Was there any part of the week's visit that you felt was really useless to you?

What poem did your poet read that stays with you? (You don't have to have a particular title, just something to help us identify the poem.)

Do you believe that this program will have a continuing impact on you?

APPENDIX B
General Requirements of Poets and Evaluation Forms

Letter to Poets

October   1972

Dear

Please read all of the enclosed information carefully. A lot of information you need to know is in the guidelines mailed to the schools. Rather than repeat this in your package I have included that mailing for you to read. (Your guidelines are not included in their mailing.) If you have any questions call me or bring them with you to Raleigh.

The dates of visits are usually the dates requested by the schools and matched with requests from the poets. These dates can be changed only through an act of me accompanied by great wailing and gnashing of teeth.

Please note that the conference date is November 3 in Raleigh and that you will be paid mileage. This is an essential meeting as your school representatives are required by the State Department to be there and they will all be hoping for a get together with their poet to arrange schedules and make plans. Note also that the poetry reading will be in the afternoon this year. Please bring a few poems to read.

Your schedule should come in to you three weeks in advance of a visit to a school. If you have any questions or it just doesn't suit you, then call me. Sometimes it might be easier for me to deal with problems since I don't have to go to the school and work for a week with whomever devised the schedule in question.

I am here this year to be of as much help as possible, so please call me if you run into any difficulty.

Best regards,

(Mrs.) Ardis Kimzey, Coordinator
Poetry-in-the-Schools Program
Division of Cultural Arts
Telephone: 829-7467

PLEASE ACKNOWLEDGE THIS MAILING

Assignment Sheet

Dear_____:
You have been assigned to:

_____School

_____Principal

_____Dates

_____Poetry Chairman

Poet's Guidelines

GENERAL REQUIREMENTS:
POETS
(Each of these is outlined in detail on following pages)

1. Participate in Poetry-in-the-Schools conference in Raleigh on November 3.

2. Help compile a booklet of student work in your school.

3. Teach four hours a day, hold one teacher conference, and give one reading if requested.

4. Send expense account to state office.

5. Send in evaluation at end of teaching week.

1. **Poetry-in-the-Schools Conference**
   See separate sheet for details.

2. **Booklets**
   Poets can mark the poems that they definitely want to appear in the booklet (and do any slight editing necessary) at the end of each day. Friday's work can be marked during the day or mailed back to the school later.

   The teacher chairman of the visit is responsible for checking the role as she (or he) compiles the booklet, making sure that each student in the poetry classes is represented. She should include at least one poem by any student who is not represented. She may also add any additional poems that she'd like to see included in the booklet. Copies of these poems have to be sent by us to the federal office. They are also the material from which the student anthology is compiled. Please give us as much choice as possible and do have the students put their names and grade levels on the work if you can do so without seeming too academic. If not, then make sure the teachers do this.

   I have asked the schools to send these in three weeks after your departure. We will need two copies here and I have asked the schools to send two copies to the poets. Please mark one of these copies as to the poems you'd like to see in the state anthology, mail it to me and these requests will be honored as much as possible.

3. **Teaching Plans and Schedules**
   See school sheets for this information.

   The specified four hours of teaching is for your protection. If you are in super shape and want to work more and the situation calls for it then feel free to do so. We put this limit on hours because last year some schools had the poet lined up for classes six hours a day and the poet could see no way to cut down on the classes without making somebody mad.

4. **Expenses**
   Enclosed you will find expense forms made up especially for the program this year. Please fill out and sign two copies for each working week. Look at the sample copy to see how it's done. Ideally there should be no expenses except mileage, lodging, food, plus the $150 stipend. The other $100 will be given to you by the school at the end of the teaching week. If you have any questions about what is allowed and what isn't it would be best to call me before you put your money

down and then can't get it back. The maximum allowed for lodging and food is $17.50 per day, and that does not include mileage. It is necessary to send in only the motel receipts.

5. Evaluations

Enclosed you will find some evaluation forms. Please send them in as soon as possible after leaving the school. We must have two copies of each evaluation.

Poet Evaluation Sheet

POETRY-IN-THE-SCHOOLS

EVALUATION: POET

Had your school prepared for your visit? How? Can you think of anything else they could have done to help the week have more impact on the students?

Did the poetry chairperson carry out her duties and fulfill the school's obligations to the program?

Please enclose a copy of your schedule and any comments you may have on it.

Did you encounter any difficulty in the school?

What teaching techniques worked best for you?

Please list materials used such as books, films, slides.

Please list anything you do or do not like about the program and the way it is carried out. Add whatever suggestions you have that might make the program better.

Do you think the program will have a continuing impact on the students after you have left? What do you anticipate will happen?

Name _____

School Visited _____

Expense Forms

ARTIST-IN-SCHOOLS PROJECT
ESEA, Title III

EXPENSE ACCOUNT FORM

(Please fill out and sign the (2) enclosed forms)

	DATE	LODGING	MEALS	DAILY TOTAL
SUNDAY				
MONDAY				
TUESDAY				
WEDNESDAY				
THURSDAY				
FRIDAY				
			TOTAL	

The maximum per diem is $17.50. Every dollar that can be saved extends the program to more students. Please attach *motel bills* to this statement.

(Travel expense: 10¢ per mile. Shortest route home to location of service, return)

DATE	FROM	TO	MILEAGE
		TOTAL MILEAGE	
		_____ miles at 10¢ =	$

The undersigned verifies that this is an accurate statement of expenses incurred while serving in the Artist-in-Schools program. The funds requested are Federal funds and they are sought herewith in compliance with all laws governing their use.

_____
Name of Consultant

_____
Address

Expense Forms

ARTIST-IN-SCHOOLS PROJECT

ESEA, Title III

EXPENSE

ACCOUNT

FORM

(Please fill out and sign the two [2] enclosed forms)

DATE		LODGING	MEALS	DAILY TOTAL
SUNDAY	12-4	$10.00	$3.25	$13.25
MONDAY	12-5	10.00	5.75	15.75
TUESDAY	12-6	10.00	7.50	17.50
WEDNESDAY	12-7	10.00	6.75	16.75
THURSDAY	12-8	10.00	6.00	16.00
FRIDAY	12-9		2.50	2.50
			TOTAL	

181

The maximum per diem is $17.50. Every dollar that can be saved extends the program to more students. Please attach *motel bills* to this statement.

(Travel expense: 10¢ per mile. Shortest route home to location of service, return)

DATE	FROM	TO	MILEAGE
12-4	Raleigh	Chapel Hill	40
12-5	Motel—School	School—Motel	10
12-6	Motel—School	School—Motel	10
12-7	Motel—School	School—Motel	10
12-8	Motel—School	School—Motel	10
12-9	Chapel Hill	Raleigh	40
		TOTAL MILEAGE	120

120 miles at 10¢ = *$12.00*

The undersigned verifies that this is an accurate statement of expenses incurred while serving in the Artist-in-Schools program. The funds requested are Federal funds and they are sought herewith in compliance with all laws governing their use.

_____
Name of Consultant

APPENDIX C

"Eating Crow on 'Rent-A-Poet'" and Letters to Schools Included in Anthology

BOOK WORLD

EATING CROW ON 'RENT-a-POET'
by Rod Cockshutt

About a year ago in this space, I took after the then new "Poetry in the Schools," program in which several North Carolina poets went into classrooms across the state to help encourage the youngsters writing poetry. At the time, I felt that the program funded by the National Endowment for the Arts and sponsored by the State Department of Public Instruction, was seriously flawed in organization, if not in concept.

For one thing, the selection process through which 30 or so poets were chosen for the program (which pays $250 a week for the poets' labors) seemed unabashedly incestuous and blithely unselective. In some cases, it seemed it wasn't so much what you knew about poetry (or about teaching poetry), but who you knew in the state's poetry establishment that led to selection. Some people, poets among them, are simply not cut out for teaching, regardless of their enthusiasm or good intentions. Yet, as far as I've been able to determine, prior experience in a classroom or with large groups of children was not a prerequisite for selection to this program. What's more, a few poets who have proven their teaching talents were not selected, while more than a few out-and-out novices were. It seemed to me at the time that in its first year of operation, at least, the Poetry in the Schools program could have proceeded with a little more caution and restraint.

Well, I'm happy to be able to eat some crow. You can't argue with success, and regardless of how I or anyone else feels about the way in which this program was organized and instituted, it has produced some remarkable results. The evidence is contained in a soon-to-be-available booklet, *And All I Have for Tenderness Is Words*, a sampling of some of the thousands of poems written for the program during its first year by school children across the state.

The booklet, which was edited by Raleigh poet and reviewer Ardis Kimzey, and published by the State Department of Public Instruction, will be available shortly in school libraries. Most of the poems were written in less than an hour, some of them in only a few minutes before the class bell rang. But, according to Mrs. Kimzey, editing was kept to a minimum. The poems are reproduced in the booklet in all their unvarnished, unadulterated brilliance. It all bodes well for the program which has been refunded and is now in its second year.

MUSIC

Music is like a
flower singing in
the wind. Music
is like a bird
singing to his
wife. It is
like a director
leading his
band. Music
Is soft as soft
can be. Music
is like a rose
waking up.

> Darlene Warren, Grade 4
> Moore Elementary School
> Winston-Salem

184

I WISH

I wish that little boys
  running
    jumping
      frisking
        playing Army
wouldn't have to be
  running
    bleeding
      dying
        ten years later
          Anne Tucker
          Morehead High School, Eden

JANITOR

Janitor
Strong, big
Mopping, sweeping, helping,
Always working for someone else
A man alone.
      Jimmy Britt
      Red Springs High School

Peace Is like time
You've gotta have both to have both.
      Nancy Murray
      New Hanover High School

FEELING BORED

I have a feeling,
it's a dark feeling.
I don't want to play the
games in the closet,
I don't want to go outside,
it's too hot. When I pick up my
book I can't read it thinking my
friends is on a beautiful palomino
in the beautiful graceful wind
while I'm sick in bed.

      Lea Cahoon Grade 5
      Moore Elementary School

Copy of Letter Sent to School with Anthology

Dear Principal:

Enclosed you will find a number of copies of the students' anthology which was complied as a result of last year's Poetry in the Schools program.

We would appreciate your handling the distribution of these anthologies within your school. Please keep two copies for your school library and give one to the teacher who was in charge of the poet's visit last year. One copy is enclosed for each student who is represented in the anthology. We have clipped the student names to each anthology to make it easier for you to distribute.

We understand that some students may be in other schools this year or may have moved away to other towns. We would appreciate any effort on your part to locate the student in order that he may take pride in knowing about his work selected for state-wide publication. You might also want to inform your local newspaper of the publication of your students' poems.

Thank you for your cooperation.

Best regards,

(Mrs.) Ardis Kimzey, Coordinator
Poetry-in-the-Schools Program
Division of Cultural Arts

AK:ch

APPENDIX D

Time Schedules and Explanations

SAMPLE 1: *Cross Reference Schedule*

POETS PARTICIPATING IN THE
POETRY-IN-THE-SCHOOLS PROGRAM

Adcock, Betty (Mrs.) 817 Runnymede Rd. Raleigh, N.C. 27607 (Home) (919) 787-2407	Fike High School Wilson, N.C. Sanford Central Sanford, N.C. Sparta Elem. Sparta, N.C.	Feb. 5-9, 1973 Feb. 19-23, 1973 March 5-9, 1973
Barton, Lew P.O. Box 35 Pembroke, N.C. 28372	E. Wilkes High School Ronda, N.C.	Feb. 5-9, 1973
Buckner, Sally (Mrs.) 3305 Ruffin St. Raleigh, N.C. (Home) (919) 834-8713 (Bus.) (919) 832-2881	Goldsboro High School Goldsboro, N.C.	March 12-16, 1973
Fields, Julia (Ms.) Box 209 Scotland Neck, N.C. (Home) (919) 826-4300	Independence High School Charlotte, N.C. A.L. Brown Kannapolis, N.C. High Point Central High Point, N.C.	Dec. 11-15, 1972 March 5-9, 1973 Feb. 5-9, 1973
Grey, Robert W. 4639 Munsee St. Charlotte, N.C. 28213 (Home) (704) 597-0730 (Bus.) (704) 597-2296	N. Moore High School Robbins, N.C. Jonesville School Jonesville, N.C.	March 5-9, 1973 Open

SAMPLE 2: *Cross Reference Schedule*

SCHOOLS PARTICIPATING IN THE
POETRY-IN-THE-SCHOOLS PROGRAM

CABARRUS
A.L. Brown H.S. (10-12)   Hal Sieber   March 19-23, 1973
415 E. 1st St.
Kannapolis, N.C. 28081
Byron L. King, Prin.
Jim A. Rodger, Ch.,

STANLY
Albemarle Jr. H. (7-9)   Cam Reeves   March 5-9, 1973
266 N. 3rd. St.
Albemarle, N.C. 28001
W.L. Smith, Prin.
Mrs. Ree H. Phillips, Ch.

ALLEGHANY
Alleghany High (9-12)   Tom Walters   March 5-9, 1973
Sparta, N.C. 28675
James A. Greene, Prin.
Mrs. Sarah McMillan, Ch.

TRANSYLVANIA
Brevard Elem. (1-6)   Maria Ingram   March 5-9, 1973
S. Gaston St.
Brevard, N.C. 28712
Richard Voso, Prin.
Margaret Kilstrom, Ch.

The two schedules with the cross referencing plan need a bit of explanation. I wanted some way of having all the information I would need all year at my fingertips and on my desk. This was one way of doing it and I can testify that it worked as well as anything would. I kept a desk copy of everything and kept it all up to date. There were many copies floating around that weren't accurate even after the first month, but my copy and my secretary's copy were always accurate.

The reason we have the schools listed first by county is because the schools are listed that way in the statewide directory and if we wanted to look anything up in the directory we had to have that information first. On the other hand, I listed the schools alphabetically since that was the best way for me to find them in a hurry from the desk copy. Despite the fact that we had lots of information, I still found that I should have put the phone number of the school on the sheet. During the year we did that on a separate sheet, but it would have been more efficient if we had put it on this sheet.

So we had one sheet that started with the name of the school. Then we had another sheet that was made up according to the poets who were working in the program. That had their address or addresses and phone numbers and where they were working and when. Between the two listings, we really had an easy time of it keeping up with everything and everybody. Also, at a glance I could tell anybody who called almost any information they wanted to know.

In any case both of these schedules were in the poets' packages so that they could also tell where everybody was at all times. We figured that some of them might want to travel together or get together to exchange notes if they were nearby, or even to entertain some of the poets if they landed in their hometown. We tried to put poets as close to home as possible to work, but some requested any place other than where they were from. "A prophet is without honor in his own country" and all that sort of philosophy.

APPENDIX E

An Anthology of Student Poems And Teaching Ideas

by Thomas N. Walters

Poems. Emotional human statements expressing an astonishing range of sensitivities, sensibilities. The depths of perception and subtleties of tone and color these young writers are capable of producing is inspiring to me.

Here are some "assignments," "topics," "subjects," —what you will—that I have found to work. Following each assignment are several examples of student responses to them.

Assignment #1:   "Watch television for exactly two hours. Then get by yourself and jot down a free-association poem. Put it away for two more hours. Then reread and 'refine' it."

KIDS IN THE UNIVERSE

Lightning blamed for crash...
Kids are kids, whether rural or urban,
    Said the director.
Of what?
So what?
      Body count disputed by pentagon. Body Odor
      Found offensive by man-power.

Red Hot Team destroys Sox
Kids will be kids
Destroying sox, going barefoot
To the well
With supremely-courted hair,
Books, Movies, and well-ruled so-forth.
Market drops, tear drops, tear gas hurled.
Prices rise, planes fall on plain of jars.
Generation gap. Credibility gap. General Bap.
I could not help myself, moans killer.
Kids are people kidding around
      on the edge of the paddy ditch peering down
      shooting, shooting, shooting.
Kids are kids
      whether rural or urban.
      And we are alone in the universe
        says professor.

          (a girl who called herself "Rain")
          11th grade
          Samarkand Manor Correctional School for Girls

NEWSCAST

Sitting at the desk watching TV
Was a flag being burned
But it seemed crying to me
The fire dripped like tears
Or dripped like blood
Down below to the slithering mud.

          Heather—11th grade
          Samarkand Manor

"WHAT I SEE"

The letter C reminds me
      of a half of an egg.
A light bulb reminds me
      of the sun showing through

the glass.
The letter Q reminds me of a man
    with a cigar
    hanging out of his mouth.
The stars in the sky
    remind me of the
    Dallas Cowboys.
The word crazy is like
    my dog.

                    Dwight Bryant—8th grade
                    Millbrook Jr. High

COMMERCIALS

Today's TV commercials are really
Going mad.
With some silly thing that really
Can't be compared.
For instance the lady who washes
Her hair in Breck
Only to find out later it
Looks like a wreck.
Or the man who uses Scope
But finds out he also needs to use soap.
These are only samples of trade
Productions
With crazy TV commercials, they
Need no introductions.

                    Diane—10th grade
                    Samarkand Manor

FLIGHT

Off into the unknown
soars the wings of man,
The world is flying by me
and looks like a spinning ball
Suddenly, the jet soars
down to earth,
and has ended the flight

192

of man.
The sleek jet waits
for its next flight.

David Peed—8th grade
Millbrook Jr. High

EARTH FRIEND
(For Jacques Cousteau)

The sea is my friend,
It's the loneliest of
        my friends.
People don't care about
        it.
They use it for a trash
Dump and a sewage plant,
It's a bummer to watch,
People do this to my friends.
Why do they do this to my friends?
One day they will regret that
They did this to my friends!!!
They are using up all
The trees and polluting the
Rivers but most of all
They are developing the
Marshes that will cut a
Lot of my little friends out.
This is truly a sad sight!!!

Kenny Pearce—8th grade
Millbrook Jr. High

PEOPLE OF THE WORLD

With all your rich personalities twostepping
With all your Nazi and neofascist goosestepping
With all your farmers feeding his sucklings

193

With all your comedians chuckling
With all your nonsense you are
all alike.

Frank Isley—11th grade
J.M. Morehead High
Eden, N.C.

SUNDAY MORNING SERVICE

Mouths move in uncomprehending reflection
Minds ponder the time of day
Children cry, mothers pamper
Preachers read bought sermons
Choirboys play games
"This is the way we worship the Lord, worship
      the Lord, worship the Lord, this is the way...

Robin Paisley—11th grade
Alleghany High

Assignment #2: "Tell us something new about what you are—or what someone else is—or what you (or they) might prefer to be."

SKY STUDY

Have you ever wanted to glide as freely and
undisturbed as the gulls above the restless waters
To sail higher and smoother through the sunburst sky
That perhaps is me.

Becky Boyte—12th grade
J.M. Morehead High

194

THIS RACIAL THING

How long will it last
How far will it go
This racial thing, you know.

You can't be my friend, sister or brother
Because of the way your skin is colored.
You have this tan
You say it's an outward expression
Of your fellowman.

My skin is black, yours is white
Let's join hands and make
This world right.
This color I inherited
From the long dark continent
Of Africa.

> Taminika—10th grade
> Samarkand Manor

"TO FIND ME"

Who am I?
I am the number of friends I have
Divided by the people whose friend
I am.
To check your work,
Take the whole world
And subtract everybody else;
I'm what's left.

> Mike Edwards—11th grade
> ·J.M. Morehead High

HIPPOCRITICAL HYPOTHETICAL HYPOTENUSE

Because you're glad you're not the longest
side of a *wrong* triangle
You assume your role to be correct
Just as novice mathematicians

"assume" the theorems they attempt.
You are Eohippus. A beginner and
very small. The three corners
of your life can't all be
right Angles.
Times change ideas of life...
and of living. Don't forget—
that without your individual
corners you'd be a circle.
Sort of round and very uncertain.

Beth Bradford—11th grade
J.M. Morehead High

WHAT I AM AND THINK

I am two in one
one is reflection,
the other an image
I need to find where I belong
for I am lost.

I'm lost in the thought,
of a hillside of green grass.
I belong in the country,
where I am free.
I want to be where I
can find peace.

There is a difference in,
everyone on earth.
We look and want everything,
that comes by.
But here I sit dreaming
of a green hillside.

Jimm McIntyre—8th grade
Millbrook Jr. High

196

WONDERING

I wished I was a flag. Then
I would be pretty high. But
I don't know I wouldn't be
Able to look at television
Laugh or sing.
I wonder if
Flags giggle, and how they
Use a desk, I bet they don't
Even try to dress, they wear
The same stars and stripes over
And over again. I guess I like
To be just how I am.

Donna—11th grade
Samarkand Manor

"THE WIND"

I am the whispering wind kissing love's blush
    onto the cheeks of spring
Like the fragrant breath of God unseen but blessing
    the grass to bend in meadows,
        to grow
            in concrete streets
    where I turn the knife, the gun—
        all things hatred
          into peaces
Of pleasures like the flutter of whirling pigeons
    flying, living, loving,
Whispering to tall trees, tall buildings,
    my special people beneath them,
The joy of being and just letting be.

Rachel Creech—12th grade
J.M. Morehead High

MUCH LOVED ONES

If the song you sing
Is set to another man's tune
Pass me by.

197

My fields would be no richer
After having been crossed by you.
And if the petals of my soul were shed upon you,
You would probably just sit and cock your head,
Looking puzzled
The way my cocker spaniel used to
When he heard a noise he didn't understand.

If your carol to the stars
Is your own,
If you have a burning desire
That the poor world might taste
The sweet honey you've found
Then venture to stay with me awhile.
Perhaps you will find me worthy
Of sharing your silver
And perhaps I can give you a taste
Of my wine.
Entangled in each other and separated by the winds,
Let us follow the treasure map until we reach the X.

For I am a seeker of knowledge
And an admirer of that which is genuine
And true.

Joy Roupe—12th grade
Alleghany High

BESIDES...

Where do I belong?
Here or there?
No matter where
There's always somebody
Who—
Who what?
Do I know?
Do you?
Never mind.

Don't tell.
It will be too complicated.
Besides I'd rather dream my
Own dreams.

Heather and Rain—11th grade
Samarkand Manor

LOVE POEM

When you and I began,
　　The I ended.
Becoming us—we became you.
I was lost, destroyed, ignored.
As you opened yourself in me, I remained
　　closed within you.
Drawers in me were shut—
　　flowing emotions frozen,
Why cannot we be we?
　　　With you I am not.
　　　With me alone, I am.

Kathy Greene—11th grade
Alleghany High

GROWING UP

The air dances with meaningless
　　Words and
　　Faceless mouths
　　Sings nothings.

But I'm an actor,
　　I pretend.
Pictures flush and fade my face
As I sit with eyes
Lit and expression intense,
　　　Inside.　.　.
　　　　　Empty
But I am an actor, I pretend.
Perhaps I am growing up.

Linda—11th grade
Samarkand Manor

Assignment #3: "Show us an image of some thing, some one, or a situation we've already seen. But make us *see* it for the 'first' time, now."

KILLERS

PT boats fly
Water curves back from bow
torpedoes try to strike hard
but fail.

> Joe Snow—8th grade
> Millbrook Jr. High

THE PENCIL SHARPENER

I feed him my pencil; he hungrily churns;
Grinding and gnawing with each greedy turn,

Gulping his diet of shavings and lead,
Anxiously waiting again to be fed.

> Lynne Price—11th grade
> Samarkand Manor

THE TRIP

Once upon a time in Training School
Lived a girl they called Louise the fool
For she believed she could sit in
Trees and blow wild and that
The blue blotches with plastic
Badges
Couldn't reach her when she
Was that high
But that arm of injustice
Wrapped around her neck
Squeezing and strangling and forcing out
All that she believed and cared about.
Dragging her down to their world
They put her in a cage with
Padded walls.
She sits and remembers how
Life used to be.

200

She thinks there is some good
Left in the world.
And you know something?
SHE'S WRONG.

Rain and Heather—11th grade
Samarkand Manor

THE FLYING ZEBRA

The butterfly is leaf size
But yet so large
It is like a zebra with wings
but smaller.
The zebra lives on the ground
But the butterfly loves the air
    The zebra is born a zebra
    But the butterfly is born a caterpillar.

Ricky Young—8th grade
Millbrook Jr. High

SITTING DOWN ON SAMARKAND

Sitting down on Samarkand,
It's not so bad and it's not so good,
It's just the way you look at it.
But when you get there
You will not like it at first.
You may cry one or two times
And then you will not cry again
Till you hear a sad song
Then you will be wanting to go home
And soon you go home for good
Samarkand is not a bad name
But if you want to come here
Just say Samarkand Manor
Where all the girls work hard
And cry deep down in their sleep.

Annie—10th grade
Samarkand Manor

THE STORY

I was sitting on the edge of my pool
Washing my hair
Feeling the sun
Getting ready to curl it,
When the rain came
And I dropped my radio into the pool.

Kathy—10th grade
Samarkand Manor

THE FOX

He attacks his victim with a great leap,
    Sinking his teeth into cold,
        shivering flesh.

Ripping and
    Tearing till he has what he
        longed for

And leaving,
    Eating the woods slowly with his feet
        searching for another
            victim.

Anne Beal—11th grade
Millbrook Jr. High

WHAT DOES THE RAIN MAKE?

The rain
as it hits ground
splashes against the wall
like the wind blowing dirt around
makes mud.

Tammy Walser—8th grade
Millbrook Jr. High

SNAKE

A snake is like a crooked branch,
With strange greenbrown bark,
Always lying silently alone,
Apart from the rest of the world,
Always quiet, dry, listening.

Vicki—10th grade
Samarkand Manor

CHRISTINA'S WORLD

I am blind and cannot see
I struggle so hard, but somehow I always seem
to fail.
I am lost in a lonely field and no one's even close
to me.
I feel the grass below my hand all coarse and rough.
The sky is dark, cold, and lonely feeling.
The ground is hard and cold beneath the place
I lie.
I wish one least something would turn on suns
of light in my life.

Kim Edwards—8th grade
Millbrook Jr. High

LEVELS

A weak person is like a lake...
    Forever shifting levels.

Linda Wilkerson—12th grade
J. M. Morehead High

SPRING

Spring is like dancing and prancing
                on the grass,
Then sit down by the spring
And put your tired feet in it and rest,
And a butterfly comes
                and sits down in your lap.

Lynne Price—10th grade
J. M. Morehead High

MOTORCYCLE

I'm riding down the beach.
 Swaying from side
                      to
                           side.
With the wind in my face,
Pushing me back.
The dirt swinging beneath
my wheels, speeding down
the beach.

                    Greg Costa—8th grade
                    Millbrook Jr. High

Motorcycle traveling fast like the wind
and a H
         I
           G
            H
              W
                A
                 Y
looks like spaghetti. When you're in a
plane. See you there in a lane. Then
you and me will be free.

                    David Barbour—8th grade
                    Millbrook Jr. High

Assignment #4:   "Write about a personality, object, or idea and make
                    a word-play which makes us think—or re-think—
                    about the word's meaning."

ForkShiver

The spaghetti of my love
was sent from a pot
to be captured by
your fork only.

Just the thought of your lips
Caressing my tomato sauce
Sends shivers through
My American cheese.

Heather and Rain—11th grade
Samarkand Manor

MEDITATION

A swelling crescendo
of empty voices
stuffs nothings into
cluttered minds, smothering
thoughts we have nourished
and nursed—
blinding us from what is true
or ours.

Lynne—11th grade
Samarkand Manor

ALIKE, BUT DIFFERENT

Maria Tallchief dances with her
    own grace and beauty,
Like the tall chief of the Indians dances
    with his own warlike splendor.

And as the tall Chief of Police dances
    through his turmoil and sweat of every day,
So does Maria dance through the
    sweat of each movement of her person.

Debra Orris—12th grade
J. M. Morehead High

ODE TO CHILDHOOD: IN A LATER MARKET

Where are the carefree days I once knew?
Of Raggedy-Ann and Skip-to-my-Lou?
Of jump ropes and hopscotch games?
Of beautiful dolls with enticing names?
Of Easter Bunny and Santa Claus?

Of merry-go-rounds and bouncing balls?
Where are those carefree days I once knew?
One spring day a trade wind blew.

Paige Morehead—12th grade
J. M. Morehead High

WORD GAME

Sandwiched between cool sheets I rest
defenseless against archaic thoughts 5 or 6
hours out of every 24.
Images worm their way through
the brain, the giant caterpillar who lurks behind
my eyes.
Visions and sounds in black
and white
lead my nocturnal wanderings until dawn
when light bids me awaken—
and the soft riverwind of reality clears the fog–
gy sleep.

Kathy—11th grade
Samarkand Manor

FROM "A CLOCKWORK ORANGE"

Ah! Ludwig Van!
How the sweet concertos
stimulate the soul and
ease the mind—the
music's fragrance—
a soothing aroma to
the senses—
Ah! TOUCHÉ, world!

Carol Sweeney—11th grade
J. M. Morehead High

DANGER PLAY

Ol' Osiris, the ruler, of the underworld
Sits in dungeon, judging his dead,
Pronouncing their sentences, with an eerie laugh.

206

He howls at the thought of love,
Or the scent of a gleaming iris,
In the morning dew.

Jane Elrod—12th grade
J. M. Morehead High

ONE WEEK IN EDEN

Out of Barker's* calm bag:
To be becomes being and is;
Add am to the verb and think was;
Tack an eve onto the we of us
to begin the good times had.
These days farther west than
    Steinbeck nodding got
Have given us, the motley crew,
More heart, more head than we
    ever knew.
New faces, new laughter, new dreams
Come on bright, and the leaving
    is tough. America a world
    Awaits these spirits.

—Thomas Walters

*Miss Betty Barker, a marvelous teacher at J. M. Morehead High School in Eden, N.C. She edited the student magazine in which this poem appeared on the dedication page. I wrote it for a class there as an illustration of plays on words, as well as a tribute to the students and their talents.

KENYA

Ken-ya col-on-ee
Ken-ya call on me?
Ken-ya love?
Ken-ya accept?
Ken-ya be?
Ken-ya, Ken-ya,
Ken-ya be?
      Ken-Ya??

Linda Wilkerson—12th grade
J. M. Morehead High

Assignment #5: "Write a poem—not a love poem—about someone you care about, a friend or an acquaintance."

PATTERNS

Our lives are like the macrame
    that Robert does so well.
Just as he sits and weaves belts
    by the hour
So do we weave our dreams
    by the years.
But Robert will finish his belts
    and hang them in the store
    to sell.
While ours is a never ending task...
Stars and moons and suns
Are for hanging dreams
    upon,
And dreams are no so easily sold
    at
        half-price.

                Kathy—11th grade
                Samarkand Manor

WAITING

From her hidden corner, the woman watches
As the slithering Casanova
Moves through the bustling crowd,
Past the booth
With his smooth, suave Bossa Nova movement.
Could he be the one?

                Linda—11th grade
                Samarkand Manor

THIS MAN I KNOW
(for TW)

I can vision him now;
Standing as high as the
Pine tree
Courageous as the

208

Fighting bull,
More fierce than
Any known in history
But yet I vision this man
As gently as the wind
Blowing softly
As peaceful as the
Still water
And kindness showing more than
The kindness he has ever known.

Dorothy—11th grade
Samarkand Manor

LOSS

When my friend was
near, I felt secure. But
now she has gone so very
far.

She sails wherever
the golden wind blows, with
the birds showing the way
    over-
        head.

Kenny Pearce—8th grade
Millbrook Jr. High

the jive poet
(for TW)

a celebrity figure
with a conforming style
gazing through his golden specs
muttering "oh, hell."

impressive in works
sophisticated in knowledge
using the folksy approach
to stimulate our inners.

tom we preferred to call
but rarely used
while he jived around
superbad and supercool.

"be a child"
"say the opposite of meaning"
"be modern"
"but be you"

a poem i attempt
but stunned i become
until he says
"oh, hell just be yourself."

Linda Wilkerson—12th grade
J. M. Morehead High

HIS EYES

His eyes show pain,
A sparkling tear.

He cannot cry.
He must be strong;
He should not fear;
I will not leave.

Somehow he knows
And shares my joy.
I pity him.

His eyes can't see:
They told me so.
His lifeless eyes.

Dawn Shropshire—12th grade
J. M. Morehead High

SUPERANNUATION

I saw him once just the other day.
He was all alone, sitting on a bench;
And my impulse was to forget him.
Yet—I couldn't. He was no different
From any other old man—but he was.
He kept haunting me, his face returning
So vividly that I could see every detail—
The shock of white hair, the lined, weather-beaten
Face, the time-worn smile, and his eyes—

His deep, startlingly blue eyes
That so painstakingly reflected the sorrow
And solitude of a person forgotten
And lost in a changing world.

Kimberly Hicks—8th grade
Millbrook Jr. High

LONELY YOU

There are so many people
Going their own way.
They hurry by without
Anything to say.

Even in this big old world
People are so sad.
Cause there isn't much love
And that's something they've never had.

Loneliness is like eating an apple
Dropping it on the road
Never to taste the same apple again.

Loneliness is seeing your future in a dream,
And knowing you can't change it.

Linda—11th grade
Samarkand Manor

Teachers & Writers Publications

THE WHOLE WORD CATALOGUE 1 (72 pages) is a practical collection of assignments for stimulating student writing, designed for both elementary and secondary students. Activities designed as catalysts for classroom exercises include: personal writing, collective novels, diagram stories, fables, spoof and parodies, and language games. It also contains an annotated bibliography.

THE WHOLE WORD CATALOGUE 2 edited by Bill Zavatsky and Ron Padgett (350 pages). A completely new collection of writing and art ideas for the elementary, secondary, and college classroom. Deepens and widens the educational ground broken by our underground best seller, the first *Whole Word Catalogue.* Order two copies and get a free subscription for a friend.

IMAGINARY WORLDS (110 pages) originated from Richard Murphy's desire to find themes of sufficient breadth and interest to allow sustained, independent writing by students. Children invented their own Utopias of time and place, invented their own religions, new ways of fighting wars, different schools. They produced a great deal of extraordinary writing, much of it reprinted in the book.

A DAY DREAM I HAD AT NIGHT (120 pages) is a collection of oral literature from children who were not learning to read well or write competently or feel any real sense of satisfaction in school. The author, Roger Landrum, working in collaboration with two elementary school teachers, made class readers out of the children's own work.

FIVE TALES OF ADVENTURE (119 pages) is a new collection of short novels written by children at a Manhattan elementary school. The stories cover a wide range of styles and interests—a family mystery, an urban satire, a Himalayan adventure, a sci-fi spoof, and a tale of murder and retribution.

TEACHING AND WRITING POPULAR FICTION: HORROR, ADVENTURE, MYSTERY AND ROMANCE IN THE AMERICAN CLASSROOM by Karen Hubert (236 pages). A new step-by-step guide on using the different literary genres to help students to write, based on the author's intensive workshops conducted for Teachers & Writers in elementary and secondary schools. Ms. Hubert explores the psychological necessities of each genre and discusses the various ways of tailoring each one to individual students. Includes hundreds of "recipes" to be used as story starters, with an anthology of student work to show the exciting results possible.

JUST WRITING by Bill Bernhardt. A book of exercises designed to make the reader aware of all the necessary steps in the writing process. This book can be used as a do-it-yourself writing course. It is also an invaluable resource for writing teachers.

TO DEFEND A FORM by Ardis Kimzey. Tells the inside story of administering a poets-in-the-schools program. It is full of helpful procedures that will insure a smoothly running program. The book also contains many classroom-tested ideas to launch kids into poetry writing and an extensive bibliography of poetry anthologies and related material indispensable to anyone who teaches poetry.

BEING WITH CHILDREN, a book by Phillip Lopate, whose articles have appeared regularly in our magazine, is based on his work as project coordinator for Teachers & Writers Collaborative at P.S. 75 in Manhattan. Herb Kohl writes: "There is no other book that I know that combines the personal and the practical so well. . . ." *Being With Children* is published by Doubleday at $7.95. It is available through Teachers & Writers Collaborative for $7.00. Paperback $1.95.

TEACHERS & WRITERS Magazine, issued three times a year, draws together the experience and ideas of the writers and other artists who conduct T & W workshops in schools and community groups. A typical issue contains excerpts from the detailed work diaries and articles of the artists, along with the works of the students and outside contributions.

☐ The Whole Word Catalogue 2 @ $6.95
☐ The Whole Word Catalogue 1 @ $4.00
☐ Teaching & Writing Popular Fiction @ $4.00
☐ Being With Children @ $7.00 ☐ $1.95 (Paper)
☐ Five Tales of Adventure @ $3.00 (10 copies or more @ $2.00)
☐ Imaginary Worlds @ $3.00
☐ A Day Dream I Had at Night @ $3.00
☐ Just Writing @ $4.00
☐ To Defend a Form @ $4.00
☐ Subscription(s) to **T&W Magazine**, three issues $5.00, six issues $9.00, nine issues $12.00

NAME _____

ADDRESS_____

☐ I am ordering two copies of **The Whole Word Catalogue 2.** Please send a free subscription to the name and address listed below.

NAME _____

ADDRESS_____

☐ Please make checks payable to Teachers & Writers Collaborative, and send to:
   Teachers & Writers   TOTAL
   186 West 4th Street   ENCLOSED
   New York City 10014 $_____